RANDOM
HOUSE

LARGE
PRINT

Vacationland

John Hodgman

Vacationland

True Stories from Painful Beaches

~

RANDOM HOUSE
LARGE PRINT

Published in the United States of America by Random House Large Print in association with Viking, an imprint of Penguin Random House LLC, New York.

Cover design and illustrations by Aaron James Draplin, Draplin Design Co.

The Library of Congress has established a Cataloging-in-Publication record for this title.

ISBN: 978-0-5255-0124-4

www.randomhouse.com/largeprint

FIRST LARGE PRINT EDITION

Printed in the United States of America

10 9 8 7 6 5 4 3 2 1

This Large Print edition published in accord with the standards of the N.A.V.H.

For Eileen Callahan Hodgman

~

CONTENTS

The
Beginning

~

The Bookkeeper for the Church of Satan

I apologize for my beard. Not only because it is terrible—thin, patchy, and asymmetrical—but also because it is inexplicable. Many people have asked me why I grew it, and most of those people are my wife, and to them and to her I say: I don't know. I'm sorry.

Before my beard I just had a mustache, and that was not mysterious at all. In fact, I have grown two mustaches in my life, for equally banal, emotionally transparent reasons. I grew the first one in 1999, in the yearlong run-up to my marriage to the woman who is still my wife. I had only ever been clean-shaven before then (aside from an obligatory early-'90s flirtation with a soul patch in college), and I suppose now I was testing her. A few very good-looking people I know turn mean when they drink, mocking and abusing the people who care about them. They make themselves ugly to see if people will still love them that way. I think my mustache—thick and dark and unwanted in the middle of my round pale face—served the same function: to be repulsive on purpose. I looked like a bushy nineteenth-century president who also happened to be a baby.

Luckily, my then-fiancée, whom I have known since high school and who had already seen me through various thicks and thins, did not take the bait. She did not confirm my fear that I was an unlovable fraud and did not decline to marry President Chester A. Baby. So I shaved off my mustache the morning after my bachelor weekend in a dilapidated mansion in Atlantic City that I had rented with a group of friends. I cannot remember whether this was my decision or her command. Maintaining such fogginess about free will is, I think, a secret to a lasting marriage. And ours has lasted. You have the numbers in front of you, so you can do the math. (I have never been good with subtraction, especially with odd numbers like 1999 and 2017.)

I grew my second, and currently enduring, mustache in 2011. By that time we had two children, whose actual names will never be revealed. As you know, I have always hesitated to talk about my children and, when pressed, would refer to our daughter only as

"Hodgmina" and our son as "Hodgmanillo." In the past I have said that this is to protect their privacy, and that is true of our son who is, as of this writing, still young enough to like us. There are many joys of parenting, but ultimately we are robots training our own upgrades to replace us. But my son doesn't know this yet. He doesn't know that his job is to grow and thrive apart from us and conspire with time in our destruction. He still holds our hands and does not treat us like we are hopelessly stupid and so I wish to protect him.

But Hodgmina is now a luminously smart teenager with a strong social media presence who I think would enjoy being named in this book. So I keep her anonymous to spite her. I love her. I hope of course that she will outlive me (these are the fun hopes you nurture when you are older). But I do not need to help her outpace me in fame.

Insecurely teasing a teenager is a privilege of fatherhood. And I grew my second mustache for the same reason all your weird dads grew theirs: it is an evolutionary signal that says, "I'm all done." A mustache sends a visual message to the mating population of Earth that says, "No thank you. I have procreated. My DNA is out in the world, and so I no longer deserve physical affection. Instead, it is time for me to turn away from sex and toward new pursuits, the classic weird dad hobbies such as puns, learning trivia about bridges and wars, and dreaming about societal collapse and global apocalypse."

All dads dream about the end of the world. It is a comfort to them. For some, the fantasy is blunt, vengeful, and aspirational. The zombie epidemic story, as one example, is consistently popular for a simple reason: when chaos consumes civilization, you can start over. You get to be young again. All your debts, real and emotional, are canceled. Whatever your dumb job used to be, it has now been replaced with the sole, exciting occupation of survival via crossbow or samurai sword. You get to dress up and wear armor or an eyepatch. And since your neighbors have now been transformed into the idiot monsters you always believed them to be, the zombie epidemic offers you moral permission to shoot them in the head, finally.

(This is not my fantasy, by the way. I have

often thought that if **The Walking Dead** really wanted to provoke horror, its last season would time-jump five years to a future in which the government re-forms, the zombies have been cured [aside from the ones our heroes decapitated], and all the characters have to get dumb jobs again. The humans will have to work alongside the horribly mutilated cured zombies and think about what they did to survive, and what they became, while they all sit around in the break room together with their reheated soups. That said, I don't want to sound snobby about zombies. I get it. If there were a zombie show that just featured the characters endlessly raiding supermarkets for canned goods and then stocking those cans neatly back in their compound pantry, I would watch it for nineteen seasons. Guns and power and the weird masculine redemption fantasy of white dudes getting back to running things has never meant as much to me as abundant, well-organized food.)

The apocalypse I dreamed of was different, and presented a different consolation. I was in the Pioneer Valley, in the western part of my home commonwealth of Massachusetts, an important place in my life. I was sitting in the Montague Bookmill, a used-book store inside a creaky old sawmill that looks about to collapse into the shallow little river that once powered it. It was where I had written a lot of my first two books, and I was now trying to start another. But I was having trouble because I had just realized that I was not going to live forever.

The thought had never occurred to me before. I am a straight white man, the hero of almost every story I had ever encountered. What's more, I am an only child. The idea that the world could continue without me was not only unimaginable, it was insulting. But in that moment, something shifted. I was upstairs at the Bookmill alone, sitting at a nicked wooden table before two open windows, their glass wavy with age. The door behind me was open and full of sun, the ancient eaves above me cold with summer shadow, the little river giggling outside as it slowly consumed its rocky foundation. I was halfway through my fortieth year, Mustache II in graying bloom, writing a book in a used-book store, exactly where books go to die. And then it was a physical sensation that I remember: suddenly I was gripped, just above my stomach, by the dumb, offensive truth. Everything ends. Nothing lasts. Not even John Hodgman.

This is a truth so obvious that we build whole world religions, grandly spangled with art and rituals and distracting hypocrisies, in order to avoid thinking about it. And if we do not succumb to religion or myth, we tell ourselves other wild stories to make us feel better. The story I started that day was **That Is All**, the last book I wrote before this one. It was the third in a trilogy of fake facts and invented history that I originally wrote for a general audience but had found a particular following among strange thirteen-year-olds. So I thought I would treat those kids to a comedy book about everyone on Earth dying all at once.

I know that sounds like a big literary innovation, but the truth was, the end-times were trending. Everyone was talking about how the ancient Mayans had calculated that the world would end in December 2012. I just added some other equally plausible elements: a giant ravaging swarm of stray dogs, a massive tsunami of blood, and eventually the Earth cracking in half to release the giant magical toad at its center on 12/21/12. Nothing you wouldn't find in any bad Google translation of the Book of Revelation, but it comforted me. Unlike the zombie apocalypse, global annihilation offered a different, better consolation: not that I could escape death, but that when I died, I got to take everyone else with me. I may not have been there at the beginning of creation, but I would be there to turn the lights off. It just felt right.

You may have noticed the world did not end on December 21, 2012, as the Mayans and I predicted. I blame the Mayans. Looking back, it was probably stupid to trust the math of an ancient people. Their calendars were made of stone, and they couldn't even make smooth pyramids. But on December 22, I was disappointed. Obviously I didn't actually want my wife and children and everyone else to be crushed by a giant, ancient, unspeakable god crawling across the Earth. But I hadn't really made any plans for the world **not** ending, and now I was stuck. I had lined up no work for 2013. And honestly, what more was there for me to do?

I had written a thousand pages of fake facts. It was every joke I knew how to tell, every story I had inside of me. And those pages, against all reasonable expectation based on my age, experience, neck fat, and asymmetric eyes, put me on camera next to my hero, Jon Stewart, and then in a series of ads for Apple. (I never met my other hero, Steve Jobs, because I was shy and still thought we had all the time in the world.)

I had slept in the bungalow where John Belushi died. I had sipped martinis in the East Hampton home called Grey Gardens out of glasses I found in the cupboard monogrammed "EBB" for Edith Bouvier Beale. I had been hugged by Chuck D. I had not only met the forty-fourth president of the United States (Barack Obama), but also goddamn George R. R. Martin, who sought me out at a Hollywood post-Emmy party, reached in his pocket, and handed me a coin of the Faceless Man. And if that means anything to you, then you will also find it meaningful that at the same party a year later, he reached in his pocket and handed me ANOTHER ONE.

Yes, George R. R. Martin carries around pocket caches of coins of the Faceless Man just to blow nerd-minds at parties, and I have that information because of the insanely fortunate, surreal life-beyond-imagining that had grown out of my books, my life's work; work that was now complete. Plus I had a ~~perfect,~~ beautiful, challenging wife,[1] healthy children who cared nothing for sports, and

[1] As proof of this, when she read an early draft of this book, my wife asked me not to use the word "challenging" because it is often read as "difficult and unlikable." As usual she was quite right, and what's more, she is not those things. So on the one hand her literal challenge was well founded. But come on, Kath.

She also rejected "perfect," and rightly so. That is both bad writing and a sentimental lie. So you can see I have struck that out.

I refused to strike out "beautiful."

I do not wish to reduce our marriage to a footnote. But this is not a book about marriage or family, both because I respect my loved ones' private lives, and because I am very selfish. This is a book about **me**, at what I hope is the beginning of the second half of my life and not the brief, final tenth.

(continued on next page)

I had been on **Battlestar** fucking **Galactica**. Honestly the world **should** have exploded just to punish me.

But it did not explode. The world was ending, yes, but only in the same slow dumb way it has always been. And so I suddenly had years to fill. I didn't know how many, and I didn't know how. And I had a sad guilty sense

---

I am an only child to the end, I suppose. And at the end, we all are.

I also do not wish to reduce our marriage to a footnote because I promised my publisher: no more footnotes. I went footnote crazy in my previous books and for that reason, among others of my narrative experiments and fascinations, we still have not managed to create a clean, scalable electronic version of those books that one can just read.

This is a straightforward book of straightforward stories that will flow easily into your electronic book reader and, I hope, your good estimation. So this will be the only footnote. Let its singularity speak to the importance of my wife and children and our lives together (despite all evidence here) and my gratefulness and dedication to them.

For the depth of my feelings on this subject, I will quote a famous writer speaking of his own marriage. I know my own wife will approve, because this is her favorite author.

"Sometimes I feel as though I were a diver who had ventured a little beyond the limits of safe travel under the sea and had entered the strange zone where one is said to enjoy the rapture of the deep."

Just Google it.

that filling those years would just be taking up space, hogging air and attention that, in a fair life, would be better apportioned to younger, hungrier souls.

So yeah, why **not** grow a beard? When you don't know what to do in your life, there is always the mystery of what happens if you just do nothing. What if I just stop taking care of myself? And what will come out of my face?

My beard is the answer. You cannot see it, but I must make you see it so you will know my shame. Its lushest portions gather on my neck (of course) and terminate to a devilish point on my chin. On the sides, it looks like salt-and-pepper ants climbing up and down my face. The mustache and soul patch of yore are still there, but still refusing to connect to each other or any other part of the madness, probably because they hate each other.

In the great, unmatching bald expanses of my cheeks there are strands of lone, black, tough, wiry hairs—like the kind Jeff Goldblum manifested when he first began transforming into the fly in **The Fly**. If you understand **that** reference, you will also understand this one: I look like I invented a teleportation pod and used myself as the first test subject. But what I didn't know as I locked the door and threw the switch was that I was not alone. I had not noticed that a man had snuck into the pod with me—an **actual** man with an **actual** beard; and after our molecular intermingling in the air between the first pod and the other, I am the wretched half-hirsute chimera that emerged on the other side.

I knew it would turn out this way. But I was compelled to grow it. All men, I think, wonder who the secret man that lives inside them is and whom they will meet in the mirror when they stop shaving. They wonder if that man is better than the one they know. If that elder sage or fantasy wizard or feral mountain man will be wiser than they, and when they are lost, if that dude will light up his staff and guide them through the dwarven mines and out of the wilderness.

Based on the overall effect, the secret man inside **me** is the part-time bookkeeper for the Church of Satan. I'm the guy who goes in every other Monday and goes through the ledger and complains to the Magus that they are spending too much money on red candles.

"And what is this? Thirty-five hundred dollars for **cleaning**? What was that for? The **sex magick ritual**? Jesus Christ, you guys . . . Oh! Sorry! I mean, Hail Satan!"

This is not the man I expected to live inside of me, but I am counting on him.

This is a book about me and my beard wandering through three wildernesses: the green mountains of rural western Massachusetts where I disposed of my youth, the mercilessly painful beaches of coastal Maine where I will eventually accept my death, and the haunted forest of middle age that lies between them. And here is a second apology. I will be honest with you: there are no fun fake facts in this book. While I may evade particular details and change some names in order to protect the privacy of those who did not ask to know me, the rest is all the awful truth about my dumb thoughts and feelings. I am sorry for this. It is all I have left.

Part One

~

Dump Jail

I am from Brookline, Massachusetts, but I was technically born in a hospital in Cambridge. So now you have a critical answer to many of my internet security questions. And as this book is about being honest with you for once, I will also tell you that my mother's maiden name was Callahan. Enjoy my Amazon Prime account and all my money.

But while both of these places are in the east, I have spent most of my adult life living part-time in the rural west of the commonwealth. This region is called, plausibly, "western Massachusetts," and more specifically the Pioneer Valley, which follows the Connecticut River north from Springfield and up to just south of the Vermont border. It's not a resort destination like the Berkshire Mountains, but instead the western edge of what amounts to Massachusetts flyover country. The hills are beautiful, but not breathtaking, and medium sized. They are crossed with little rivers, dotted with dead mills and foundries, and home to some little towns that are still thriving and others where not one but both of the village churches are for sale, and have been for years. Route 2 heading west to Williamstown is a scenic route called the Mohawk Trail, a former Native American trade route, and if you have a desire to see Mohawk junk souvenir shops of questionable taste and authenticity, you have your choice between the one with the giant tepee that is **maybe** still open and the rest that have been closed and abandoned for my whole life.

The valley is more fertile, home to a clutch of liberal arts colleges and rich plains of good land. The primary crop is tobacco. They grow it for two reasons: to sell as cigar wrappers, and to prove that every cliché you think you know about the North and South is probably wrong. There are also small family farms raising corn and grazing sheep and cattle. Some young utopians are growing incredible biodynamic lettuces, or roasting coffee, or brewing kombucha. Other young utopians are opening hopeful restaurants featuring these local ingredients and offering artisanal cocktail programs trying to latch on to the farm-to-table movement, the latest attempt to rescue the region from the death of small American manufacture and the opioid epidemic. These enterprises should be supported, since the food is really good, and most Boston foodies are still skipping western Massachusetts for Portland, Maine. When Anthony Bourdain came to Greenfield, the Franklin County seat, to film an episode of **Parts Unknown**, local restaurateurs relished a chance to show off their wares and maybe enjoy a huge, Guy Fieri–like post-Bourdain boom. Instead, he spent most of the time talking about the town's heartbreaking addiction to heroin.

To me the image of the Pioneer Valley is three emu eggs nestled in a basket at the Whole Foods down by the colleges. Someone—either a back-to-the-land liberal pioneer or back-to-the-wall local hoping to keep his farm—had put his money into emu ranching. Emu was the meat of the future back in the 1990s, but then the emu bubble (a real thing!) burst, leaving some poor soul with a flock of six-foot-tall sub-ostrich neo-dinosaurs with bad tempers and open head-holes for ears that couldn't be sold and were now just leaving their eggs all over the place. Emu eggs are mutant, Dr. Seussian–looking things: the size of a candlepin bowling ball with a shell that is a surreal, deep blue green. The produce guy at Whole Foods told me that a single egg will make an omelet that will serve six to eight, and with every word of that sentence I got progressively closer to barfing. Those three eggs in a basket at Whole Foods spoke the words of the Pioneer Valley into my own ear-holes: "We are desperate dreamers, and we will try anything." I don't know if anyone bought the emu eggs. I've never seen them in there again.

Soon after I left for college, my mother and father bought a house here, just south of Vermont, in a very small town. It is not a fancy house. My mom wanted something on one of the little rivers that trickle through the hill towns, but they are hard to come by, as construction near the river is banned now and the housing stock that remains sometimes gets washed away. So she settled on this house, a 1979 ranch home designed by an engineer instead of an architect, which means the one bathroom faces directly into the living room. It sits on the shady side of a hill in a sparsely populated rural community that advertises itself as a "right-to-farm" town on its sign, which means if you smell manure you are not allowed to complain. The house was inexpensive. It didn't sit on a river but a sluggish brook, which quickly turned into a mosquito bog once the beavers got at it.

It was their weekend home. They would drive two hours from Brookline on a Friday afternoon. My father would watch movies and make spaghetti and my mom would smoke cigarettes and read mystery novels and eat Stouffer's creamed chipped beef. If they went outside they'd maybe look at some old junk for sale in barns, or go to that one falling-down hotel on the Mohawk Trail that served day drinks to the snowmobilers and had those sausages that we liked. And then they'd head home. My mom knew how to live.

Over the years my girlfriend and I would visit them and enjoy the same things, including the cigarettes, very, very much. And then my girlfriend and I got married. A month later my mom was diagnosed with terminal lung cancer and eight months later she died.

My father attempted to go to the house a few times but found it emotionally unbearable, and so he offered it to us for a dollar. At the time I was a freelance writer for magazines, and I think he presumed—reasonably—that this would be my one chance to ever have an asset in my life. He asked if we could keep up with the taxes and expenses, and the answer to that was no. But I did have a dollar, and I missed my mom, so I took it.

My wife and I have now owned the house for twice as long as my mom did, and because my wife teaches high school and I am barely self-employed, we can enjoy it for long stretches of the summer and winter in the exact ways my mom and father did (movies, creamed chipped beef), but now minus the smoking. We compensate for that part with gin and Scrabble. When we had children we were forced to acknowledge that the house had an outside, and we started squinting into the sun and getting to know our neighbors, who are scattered and few. Our daughter and the daughter of the family across the street became best friends when they were three. And even now as teens Hodgmina's and her friend's brains lock together the moment they see each other, speaking a kind of twin language from morning to night while my son beats the shit out of the Penguin's goons on **Arkham Asylum** for the PlayStation 3 for the same period of time. It is an incredible privilege to give them access to such a different way and pace of life (we don't have **Arkham Asylum** in Brooklyn).

We even thought about moving there when it became clear that a family of four could not live in New York City on a teacher's income and the money earned from 750-word magazine articles on cheese and barn jackets. But then I went on television, and my father's worst fears for me receded. Thanks to television we were able to spiff up the house and finish a basement bedroom. We didn't think to move the bathroom, but we did add a deck off the kitchen offering a pretty good view of the hills and the bog when the sun is up. When darkness falls it is total, and at night before bed I check the basement and garage for serial killers. After more than a decade of this I have begun thinking they aren't going to show up. It is peaceful.

We have not been back for a while for reasons that I will explain later in this book. And this makes me anxious for all kinds of existential reasons, but also because the last time we were there I left four large contractor bags full of rotting food waste piled in the garage. This has become something of a habit of mine. It's not a responsible thing to do if you own a house or simply want to be part of civilization. It is absolutely an invitation to a raccoon heist.

But leaving the garbage to steep and decay for months on end is my system, and I have a very good reason for it, which is this: there is no garbage collection in rural western Massachusetts; so you have to drive your garbage to the dump; and I do not feel like doing that.

I never feel like going to the dump because it is a twenty-five-minute drive away, it is very rarely open, and when it **is** open, it scares me. It's not **intrinsically** scary. It's really just a small transfer station: a compound of recycling sheds and Dumpsters and barrels circling one big pit with a compactor in it. I like systems, and I enjoyed perfecting the protocol of each hole and sticky chamber, figuring out which is for redeemables and which is for cardboard and which is for **corrugated** cardboard. I will happily lose myself in the madness of small distinctions, and the fact is that sorting out your life garbage and getting rid of it is always cathartic, even if the task is merely literal and it makes your car and hands smell like old milk and beer.

Yes, the yellowing Stonehenge of refrigerators loitering by the Large Items shed was creepy: removing their doors only makes them seem **hungry** for children to crawl into them and die. But obviously they could do no harm now. And then there was the sad city of broken and abandoned toys lined up on the low concrete wall by the compactor. Parents don't want to throw their children's youth away, so they lay the evidence here like offerings and mark them "FREE" and walk away. I am sure by the end of the day they are all thrown into the hole by the men who work at the dump. But this isn't really scary: just monumentally sad. It gives you something to think forlornly about as you drive home.

No. My terror of the dump was deeper and

began the day my father handed me the keys to the house and said, "There is no garbage collection in rural western Massachusetts. You have to take the garbage to the dump."

And then he said the chilling words I will never forget: "If the men who work at the dump ask where you live, tell them that you are staying with Jackie Brown."

This is not a Quentin Tarantino reference. My father is not a big fan of the movie **Jackie Brown**. Rather he was referring to the actual person, Jackie Brown, who had been my mother's colleague in the nursing department of Beth Israel Hospital and later one of her closest friends. Jackie grew up in Greenfield at the bottom of our hill and still had a house—a small box perched over the North River she had bought with a friend—over in the neighboring town of Colrain.

My father isn't a liar. We **had** stayed with Jackie Brown many times when I was younger, the three of us going out to see Jackie and sit around and do nothing by the river. My mom and father would take the second bedroom, and I would sleep on the sofa by the cast-iron stove. She was our introduction to the area, and her house was the inspiration for my mom's half-failed quest to find her own sit-around-and-do-nothing house next to a river that ended with this house by a bog, where I stood now with my father, confused.

My father explained that the dump is not in **our** town, but the neighboring town of Colrain, and so technically we were not allowed to dump our garbage there. But it's still the nearest dump. So, should the guys at the dump ever ask, I was to tell them this lie: "I am staying with Jackie Brown in Colrain."

I did not like any of this plan. As I have mentioned, I am an only child. This makes me a member the worldwide super-smart-afraid-of-conflict-narcissist club. And let me emphasize: **afraid of conflict**. Since I had no siblings to routinely challenge/hit me and equally no interest in playing sports, I had grown up without any experience in conflict. I therefore had no reason to imagine that confrontation of **any** kind, ranging from fighting to kissing, was not probably fatal.

So I didn't want to break the rules. I loved rules. In any situation I wanted to know what all the rules were so that I could follow them,

perfectly, thus assuring not merely approval but also **love . . . from every single person on Earth.** So no, I did not like being put in a position where I would have to lie to some Dumpmen. The chance of failure seemed high, the chance of unanimous global affection ready to plummet.

I am still not sure why I didn't simply ask where we were supposed to dump our trash (the answer is: Greenfield). Perhaps on some level, for once in my life, I wanted to challenge myself. So after a long period of hoarding garbage anxiously in the garage, I would finally take a deep breath, shove it all into the rental car, and drive to the dump. As I drove I would rehearse my story. "I am staying with Jackie Brown in Colrain, I am staying with Jackie Brown in Colrain, I am staying with Jackie Brown in Colrain." I would say this out loud in the car, changing inflection and emphasis, like an actor or a schizophrenic. I'd try to sound confident. Sometimes I would yell it.

I did this for seven years: the muttering drive to the dump, the anxious preshow sorting and dumping of recycling before the moment of truth—circling up to throw the contractor bags into the big hole, all (illegally!) bearing "Town of Colrain" garbage tags, and then (illegally!) buying new tags from the Dumpmen in their little tollbooth next to the contractor, and waiting for the question, "Where do you live?" Seven years passed. My wife and I had our first child. And the Dumpmen never asked.

But then something happened: Jackie Brown died. Like my mom, Jackie was diagnosed with cancer. Like my mom, she succumbed quickly. I didn't get to say goodbye to her. Maybe I didn't try hard enough. Maybe I couldn't go through saying goodbye again, so soon. But I would be lying if I told you that in all my shock and mourning, I didn't also think to myself: **Shit. There goes my alibi**. Now what was I going to tell the Dumpmen? This is a small town, surely the Dumpmen would know soon that no one would be staying with Jackie Brown in Colrain ever again.

I had to come up with a new story. And I had to come up with it all on my own. I was a grown-up now and a homeowner. I couldn't rely on my father anymore. I was nervous, but I am a storyteller by training, so I set to work, and I did it. I came up with a new story to rehearse over and over again on the way to the dump, and this is it.

I would arrive at the dump, and the Dumpmen would say: "Where do you live?"

And I would say, "Good question, guys. And here is the answer. You know how my family and I used to stay with Jackie Brown in Colrain? Oh, maybe you don't, because **you never asked.** That seems very rude to me, because I was always ready to tell you. But let's put that behind us. Because this is a small town in rural western Massachusetts, I am sure you have heard that Jackie Brown has died. Yes, it is very sad. Now my family and I are helping to clean out her house and get it ready to sell. And this"—here I would gesture to the contractor bags—"is her **death garbage.**"

At which point they would be so reverent and ashamed that they would step aside and never doubt me again.

This story sustained me for quite a while, and my drives to the dump were peaceful.

Years passed this way. My wife and I had a second child. But by the birth of our son, my death garbage story began to expire. Jackie's house was only three rooms small: how many old magazines and mattresses and bedding and memories could we still be pulling out of it? What's more, as I became more familiar with the culture of the area, I gradually and darkly realized my story was **never** plausible. Because, I had observed, should a person die in rural western Massachusetts, you do not clean out her house and sell it. You take what you want, padlock it shut, and leave it for nature to reclaim.

By the end, I was flying blind. But even so, the Dumpmen never asked. Not for seven years, when the dump was overseen by the sunken-cheeked guy with the long cigarettes who looked like Dr. Johnny Fever; and not for the next seven years when he was replaced by the guy who looked like Larry the Cable Guy, but even so, I liked him. They were always nice, and I am sorry I never learned their names. It was only recently, after fourteen years, that I realized **they would never ask**. It finally struck me: **they do**

not care. They work at the dump. They probably are not paid well enough just to work at the dump, never mind worry about the provenance of the bags of food waste and mouse bodies you have come to throw in their hole.

Coming from Park Slope, Brooklyn, where I now live, it never occurred to me that humans, when armed with authority, no matter how small, would **not** use that power to sanctimoniously cudgel their neighbors at every opportunity. I have never joined the Park Slope Food Coop, for example. I have heard too often of the shamings that are doled out if you request that they stock the morally incorrect brand of hummus.

Even when no clear authority applies, the residents of Park Slope stand ready to scold. I once barely dodged a speeding car as it blew through a light on a residential street. I yelled at the driver to slow down (this yelling doesn't count as confrontation; he was long gone), only to be immediately yelled at myself by a woman on a bicycle for standing in the bike lane while I was yelling. We both agreed that a speeding car was our common enemy, especially right near the elementary school that my own children attended and probably hers too. But we would clamber atop the bodies of a hundred run-down children if it would help us reach the moral high ground first.

So it took me almost a decade and a half to understand that in rural western Massachusetts, at the dump, they aren't interested in humiliating you to make themselves feel better. They just want you to toss your trash and enjoy the sunny day and have a lollipop before you go. (They **always** have lollipops, by the way, a little basket of them on the windowsill of their office. They are the brand of lollipops called Dum-Dums, as if to say, "Congratulations, dum-dum: you threw your trash away.")

You would think that all this would come as a relief to me, but I actually felt worse. What happened to the rules? Had they changed, and now my trash was legal? Or was there **never** a rule against dumping across town lines? Or **was** there still a rule, but it was an unspoken rule: **the worst kind of rule.**

Whatever the case, it became clear that my father's fear was always fictional. I am certain now that the Dumpmen never, **ever** asked him where he lived either. But then, maybe twenty years ago, he woke up in the sweaty grip of a dark imagining: **What if they** do? **I don't want to go to Dump Jail. I have to come up with something to tell them! I have to craft a story, a story so good that I can pass it on to my son, like a mono-grammed wristwatch of neurosis that I can shove up his rectum!**

(That is a Quentin Tarantino reference. Not **Jackie Brown**, but **Pulp Fiction**.)

I love my father. It's not his fault that he made up a fear and, in order to make it feel more real to him, gave it to me. I was obviously built to receive it.

As a father now myself, it's sobering to think about how the smallest comments will ripple through your children's lives, with some leaving permanent warps. I wish I could tell you that is why I tell my own children not to lie to the Dumpmen. To know there is no Dump Jail. I wish I could tell you my children now throw the garbage in the hole unafraid, that they look the Dumpmen in the eye and address them by name while I watch from the car proudly (though always ready to gun the engine and abandon them should things go south). But the truth is they just sit in the car, reading Archies and surfing the internet, waiting for me to dump the bags and come back with Dum-Dums. I must console myself in the certainty that I am helping them and damaging them in other ways I cannot see.

Mongering

I don't like riding on city buses. Those things can go anywhere. There are no tracks, and their routes and stops are a collective fiction. What if something goes wrong? I am confident that even if the driver decided to try psychedelic mushrooms for the first time that morning, I would probably not die: no Hyundai or streetlight can fight a city bus, the blunt, slow, armored whales of the streets. But I **could** end up at some destination I did not choose, which to me feels almost worse.

But I am not **only** a creature of pure fear. In fact, growing up as an only child gives you a unique, stupid kind of courage, one that is doubled if you are white and well-off and well loved by parents who love each other. I had a protective confidence in my own specialness, which allowed me to, for example, grow my flat, greasy hair to my shoulders, put a black fedora on top of it, wear a bolo tie, carry a briefcase, and go to high school that way, every day.

By tenth grade I was cultivating all sorts

of loathsome affectations. I read the plays of Athol Fugard and Tom Stoppard. I played the viola, because it was less popular than the violin, and then I added the clarinet, because the saxophone seemed a cliché. It was important that I play **two** instruments so that I not get too good at either one, lest I ruin my status as a teen genius dilettante.

I do not know why I was not bullied more. I think I may have presented too many hate targets for bullies to get a bead on. One time I was standing outside WMFO, the Tufts University radio station where I had talked myself into a Friday afternoon slot. That was the sort of thing I would do. Mostly the deejays were Tufts students, appropriately. But WMFO high-mindedly kept a few slots open for "members of the community." I would guess they were supposed to go to marginalized voices, working people from the neighborhood, and local activists; not affluent high schoolers from Brookline who simply wanted to play the same Billy Bragg song over and over again. But somehow the station went for it, and now I had finished my shift and was starting the long walk to Porter Square to catch the train back home (there was a bus; I wouldn't take it). A car full of angry townies pulled up alongside me. They stared hard at me for a while. The one guy's dull, watery eyes searched me up and down as if to say, **Where do I begin with this specimen?** Finally he barked, "Liberal!" and they peeled out. That was the best he could do. It was fine. I really couldn't argue with them. My father had once worked for Mike Dukakis.

I was accused of being a "fag" maybe only three times, which, for Massachusetts in the 1980s, was an accomplishment. And one of those times the accusation was actually a kindness. I was having lunch with my close friend Jason, and he asked if I was gay. "Everyone is wondering," he said. "You don't seem to have any interest in girls and you dress like **Doctor Who**." I had to admit it made sense. But I wasn't gay, I told him. I felt bad about it. It might have made me more interesting.

Of course Jason **was** gay, but I didn't figure that obvious subtext out until years later, because I was purposefully stupid on such subjects. The truth was that all hugging and kissing matters made me uncomfortable. What I really wanted was to skip adolescence altogether and jump to the life of a sexless middle-aged bachelor that I yearned for. And I succeeded.

Both of my parents were the first of their families to go to college, Boston College, where they met. My father grew up in Fitchburg, Massachusetts. His father worked in a paper mill until he retired to a life of cribbage and long stretches of silence. My grandfather converted to Catholicism to marry my Italian American grandmother, who made good spaghetti sauce and sang "Tiny Bubbles" frequently. Her sisters, one widowed, the other never married, lived across the street, where they collected cats and suspected that someone was sneaking in and stealing the copper pipes in the basement and replacing them with perfect non-copper replicas. (This was not happening.)

My mom grew up in Philadelphia. She had one younger brother for a while until her parents felt guilty for using birth control and quickly had five more daughters (Catholics!),

all in a three-bedroom row home in northeast
Philadelphia. Though she loved her family,
she reversed course when she and my father
married and settled into their careers: she
became an atheist, had only one child, and
moved our tiny family into an **enormous**
house, twenty-two beautiful, crumbling rooms
that had most recently been a commune.
My mom fixed up much of it herself, and to
afford it, she rented whole floors and wings
out to graduate students and young doctors.
Even then we had more house than we could
possibly need, and the three of us would wan-
der around it, only occasionally bumping into
one another.

Only children have a special relationship
with their parents if they aren't divorced.
You're alone together in the big house of the
world, and you quickly come to rely on each
other for company as much as anything else.
You spend a lot of time traveling, going to
movies, watching **Brideshead Revisited** with
your dinners on your laps. Pretty soon you **all**
feel like boarders: they are not so much your
parents as your weird older roommates.

I was fourteen when a nursing colleague

of my mom's who had been renting some rooms in the house moved out. Her area was sectioned off with its own bathroom, living room, bedroom, even a foyer. It was perfect. I announced my intention to give up my own perfectly spacious bedroom that I had never had to share with anyone, ever, and move into what amounted to a secret apartment within my childhood home. After all, I was in high school now. I deserved it.

My parents did not object to this land grab. Maybe they didn't hear me from the other side of the dining room when I proposed it to them. Either way I began setting up my new life. I took apart my old bunk bed (all only children have bunk beds, of course. They sleep on the top bunk to at once embody their surfeit of resources and lit-eralize their loneliness: the empty, siblingless space that follows them, even to bed). I ar-ranged the top and bottom bunks into an L in my new living room, adding some corduroy-upholstered bolster pillows to make a kind of loungy sectional. I scavenged a green shaded library lamp and an old school desk and I put a manual typewriter on top of it so I could type all my thoughts. I had a fern. A **fern**. I still don't remember where that came from. They were everywhere in the '80s, I guess.

An old steamer trunk from some sub-attic was my coffee table. I put my parents' old black-and-white television on top of it, and there I would retire of an evening to watch **TV's Bloopers and Practical Jokes**, swirling a snifter glass of whole milk and simply **murdering** an entire box of Triscuits: a sophisticate.

And from that home base I would go out and explore the semi-metropolises of Boston and Cambridge and suck the thin marrow from their bones. I would go to cafés and read Julio Cortázar alone. I would peruse the early work of Nik Kershaw at Planet Records in Kenmore Square. I would go to the first Newbury Comics and be scared by photographs of Wendy O. Williams and purchase Art Spiegelman's **Raw**. At a midday animation festival at the Off the Wall cinema in Central Square, I saw "Vincent," the first short by a then-unknown Tim Burton. "That young man is going places," I said to nobody, because I was alone.

One time, coming home on the Red Line from Harvard Square, I was unwrapping a new cassette I had picked up at the Harvard Coop, an anthology of jazz violin. A young woman next to me said, "Oh, I have that! It's great."

"Good," I said, and **nothing else**. I put on my headphones and stared straight ahead. Because as much as I wanted credit for making myself into such a fascinating fake-adult, on some level even I knew I was a pretentious weirdo and she would be better off not talking to me.

I had no curfew. My parents both bought my grown-up act and saw through it for its sad yearning. What kind of trouble was **I** going to get in? Worst-case scenario, I might see some provocative installation art. And so I traveled out and back, day and night, fearlessly. And I would do this all by train and **not by bus**, because if your train conductor does shrooms in the morning, you will probably die. But you will die **on the way**, between two well-defined stops. It's not risk I am afraid of. It is **ambiguity**. On those trains, I knew where I was going.

When I became an actual physical adult, it was terrible. After high school I went to Yale. If you are not convinced of what an easy time I've had of it, witness this: I took no loans and needed no financial aid. My parents had saved assiduously and I punished their good deed by studying literary theory. Not **literature**—that would be too practical. I was less interested in books than I was in the **concept** of books. That is still true.

I mentioned that my mom was a nurse. That makes sense. But even now I have a hard time explaining what my father did during his long and obviously successful career. I know he was an executive at an early computer company. Later he oversaw a state-backed fund that invested in local emerging tech companies.

I am just using my brain to force my fingers to type those words. I never really understood what they translated to in how he spent his time, whom he worked with, how he felt about it. "My father is a businessman doing business things for businesses," was always my best guess, even now that he is retired. When I went to college to spend the money that he and his mystery occupation had raised on my behalf, he asked that I take one course in bookkeeping. It was his only request: that I take a moment to peer into his world. Of course I didn't do it. I'm sorry, Dad.

Instead I read historic comic strips as literature and worked at a video store and lived in a basement. I went to London for one semester on a drink-abroad program of my own devising and got a job at a cheesemonger's. I loved mongering. I would turn the cheeses over once in the morning and once in the afternoon (to keep their moisture evenly distributed) and between those times I would stand outside waiting for midday, when the beautiful French teenagers would descend from the École Français at the top of the street to pillage the neighborhood for warm hunks of bread and massive chocolate bars. Even their acne was beautiful.

I liked Yale because its architecture was majestic and historic and largely fictional. On the tour for prospective students I was informed that all the Gothic castles and redbrick Georgian piles that made up the campus were designed at the same time, an imitation of the slow architectural accretions of Oxford and Cambridge. The shingles were buried for months, the windows purposefully broken and repaired to seem old. That is when I fell in love. It was a set: the **concept** of college. Imagine if the phony Hogwarts in the middle of the Universal Studios theme park granted degrees along with alcohol. Now you feel it.

Once I went to a party in a Tomb. Yale was founded before the advent of the fraternity system, so the white men of generations past had to make up their own structures for sub-erotic bonding and pointless tribalism. That is why there are eighteen a cappella singing groups at Yale (more a cappella than a city the size of New Haven could ever require, though no one seems to be doing anything about it) and a half dozen or so senior secret societies, each with its own clubhouse called a Tomb, stately huge buildings that look like beautiful old public libraries with two distinctions: (1) they are completely windowless; (2) they were not built for the betterment of all society, but the secret use of, originally, small groups of wealthy eighteen-year-olds who needed privacy in which to maybe organize the secret world government but probably just drink and masturbate into a coffin.

Skull and Bones is the most famous of these secret societies, particularly for the illuminati-meets-onanism angle. But I was not invited to that one. I was invited to Book and Snake. But you dance with the secret society that brought you, I always say, and I was excited to see inside this blank, sepulchral temple to historic white privilege and take its secrets into my eye-holes. And I did it, though I don't remember what I saw. Reports from contemporaries confirm that I did make it inside the building and all the way to the top of the stairs; but the luminous truth that pulsed there (plus a fair amount of grain alcohol I had consumed at a small, pre–secret society tailgate I hosted) overwhelmed me. I fell backward down the stairs, where my head hit a portion of floor that grabbed whatever I saw out of my brain and returned it to the void. I woke up in the hospital with no memory of ever going inside. Secret societies know how to keep their secrets.

It was the first time my actions had made my parents cry. I listened to them crying on the pay phone of the Cross Campus Library. I knew that they would get the ambulance bill, and I was a good boy, so I called to give them a heads-up. I could have died, they pointed out. But I hadn't.

"What did we do wrong?" my father asked, slicing me in half.

"Nothing," I said. It was a dumb question. How could they have prevented me from climbing those stairs? If anything it was their support and love that gave me the courage to climb them, to chase weird adventure and come back with stories. "You have never done anything wrong. You have done everything right," I said. And I was crying too now. Because I knew I had fallen away from them, in some way, forever, but I knew that it was inevitable and also right.

This changed when I moved to New York. I did not intend to move there after graduation. I personally wanted to stay in New Haven and continue to work in the video store—a career with a future. But I was ordered to by my then-girlfriend, now-wife, who had moved there the year before with a mutual friend, and I complied. My roommate Adam and I chose our apartment based on its proximity to a bar we liked on Third Avenue. The apartment was a duplex: I slept in the living room, Adam slept on a kind of balcony above me that counted as a bedroom. The apartment began below ground. Our one window began at street level and stretched up about six feet, perfect for any stranger to stand, arms akimbo, and watch us sleep or, as would occur, pee on the bedsheet we nailed up as a curtain.

It turns out that New York had made no arrangements to receive me. No jobs were reserved for recent graduates with a degree in literary theory; no skylit garrets had been set aside in the West Village for me to think thoughts about books in. Even if New York were paying just a dime a dozen for dumb dreamers like me, the city would go bankrupt in twenty-five minutes.

I got temp work with a book publisher. My job was to tear up copies of David Mamet's **Oleanna** (fun!) and then tape down those pages onto blank sheets of printer paper and then number those sheets with a rubber stamp for reasons that are still unknown to me. You would think I would have loved it. Apart from the many, many thousands of dollars I had soaked my parents for indirectly, I had never taken a handout from them, because I loved having jobs. Aside from cheese- and video-mongering I had washed dishes in a small restaurant in Boston's Combat Zone, unloaded trucks for a furniture stockroom, doled out soup in a pseudo health-food café, and sold tickets and concessions at the Coolidge, the same art-deco movie theater I used to go to as a teenager to see Marx Brothers and samurai movies. Two smells I will never forget are the deep oil-and-aluminum-foil odor that worked into my fingers after a shift at the old ticket machine; and the tang and sizzle of the Windex as it hit the popcorn kettle. That's how we poisoned people.

I loved work because it was like travel: a chance to meet different people and inhabit their worlds. So the more tedious and unengaging the work was, the better, because it left more brainspace for observation and inquiry, and also because I'm pretty lazy.

In college I had taken a job as a traffic counter. I would sit on street corners in New

Haven early in the morning with a clipboard.
Alongside one edge of the board was a series of
numerical counters. I would count the number
of cars that went straight, left, and right
and write those numbers down on a sheet of
paper. I listened to music on the Walkman
I borrowed from my roommate without
telling him, and when the batteries wore
down, I would listen to AM radio. That's
how I first heard Rush Limbaugh and began
to understand that not everyone absolutely
agreed with me about everything. Pedestrians
passed me on their way into work and, because my second shift was at the end of the
day, on the way out as well. They thought
I had been standing there all day, and I let
them think that. Counting traffic was a mystery we could all enjoy.

Once a week I would go to a different café
or restaurant to meet a woman whose name
I forget. I would hand off my count sheets to
her, and she would tell me the intersections
I was to be stationed at the following week.
One time I asked her why we were counting
the traffic, and she said, "I have no idea." It
was perfect.

So you would think that tearing out pages and taping them down and numbering them would really be a delight. It was just like counting traffic, except inside, so I didn't have to wear three pairs of pants to keep from freezing before the sun came up. A real step up. But I couldn't enjoy it. As I stamped each page away, a growing sense ate at me that I was no longer becoming something—the perpetual state of college—but ending up as something. I didn't know what that was. I had difficulty tolerating that ambiguity. And so I grew anxious and depressed.

309.28

Soon after that I started going to therapy. Someone told me that New York University was offering talk therapy on a pay-what-you-can basis. They charged less because the therapists were all in training. It was like barber school: you show up, they randomly assign a young therapist to you, and he or she starts giving your mental health a crude, halting trim. If this does not sound appealing to you, you are wrong. You should always pay full price for a haircut, but if you have a chance to buy discount therapy you should grab it, because the markup on that shit is insane.

Just having permission to talk about yourself, to let your dumb thoughts out of your head so you can see them as they hang there in silence, is an illuminating gift. You could probably get the same effect talking to a cardboard standup of Captain Kirk. But in my case I had a real human therapist who was also a beautiful woman, only a few years older than me. You can appreciate what a boon this was to a girl-shy nerd and narcissist.

Finally, I could talk about jazz violin all day long and she was professionally obligated to listen thoughtfully and pretend to be interested. If this sounds gross and predatory, that is because it absolutely was. I am sure she sensed it. But the salutary effect was immediate. My anxiety and depression fell away almost instantly. From then on my therapy was just a weekly visit with Dr. Woman, my beautiful forced friend.

I remember telling her that I was beginning to fall asleep more easily, and the secret was to just fall asleep and not try to control every aspect of my dreams because my whole life feels like it is spinning out of control. Like, if I start dreaming that I am swinging like Batman from a grappling hook, I can just go with that rather than self-critiquing my own dream as a nerdy cliché. She nodded and inched her chair backward.

This went on happily for a couple of months. Then I received a letter. It was a single-page form from Psychotherapy Supercuts, requesting some basic address and personal information. Now, I love filling out forms. I enjoy any opportunity to create order out of disorder while also basking in the impression that someone cares about my address and middle initial (K). But there was something on this form that ruined my enjoyment of spelling my own name, a line item labeled "DIAGNOSIS." And after it, a number, filled in by hand, perhaps by Dr. Woman herself:

309.28

I didn't understand. Our therapy had barely begun. How could she have figured out **me**, the most complicated person on Earth, so quickly? And why was she speaking in code?

I brought the letter with me to our next session, and before we even sat down, I totally brandished it.

"Before I tell you about all of my fascinating feelings," I said. "Please explain something to me, if you can. What is 309.28?"

She blinked. I was crazy. She explained it was nothing, just a diagnostic code they were required to put down to process payment. She explained to me that the code comes from the **DSM: The Diagnostic Statistical Manual of Mental Disorders**. This thick book breaks down every possible mental issue and assigns them numbers, presumably so therapists could gossip about you in front of your face. There was even a copy in our therapy room, up on a shelf, thick as a phone book.

I asked her to get it down.

She said no. She told me that 309.28 was just a formality at this stage, a preliminary diagnosis. There was still a lot for us to work through, and many sessions to come. Which is of course what I wanted. But I couldn't help myself. I had just been told that my therapy had a **rule book**. And though she protested that it wasn't really relevant to my treatment, and I knew she was right, I still said, "The book, please." And she relented.

It was the fourth edition. It has since been updated, so perhaps this all has changed. But on that day, as I learned after some lengthy and dramatic page-leafing, the Dungeon Master's Guide to my mental health told me I suffered from 309.28: "Adjustment Disorder with Anxiety and Depression."

I asked Dr. Woman what "Adjustment Disorder" meant. She said it typically follows a change in life status, such as finishing college or moving to a new city. And then she leveled her gray eyes on me and closed the book, both on the code and in some ways also on me.

"It is often accompanied," she said, "by an inability to tolerate ambiguity."

There was a silence as I absorbed this. To be fair, the **DSM-IV** has its own aversion to ambiguity, having micro-categorized all of the enigmas of the mind into an OCD Dewey Decimal System (Obsessive-Compulsive Disorder, if you are obsessively wondering, is F42.2), even solving my humiliatingly simple diagnosis to two digits past the decimal. But she was right.

"Well," I said. "You are a good therapist."

"Would you like to sit down and talk now?" she said.

I did want to. But I had ruined it. I knew if I continued I would just be a creep, wasting her time. Everything was clear now.

"Good-bye," I said.

Rocks on Top of Other Rocks

There are no subways in rural western Massachusetts. There are some small commuter buses, but if you are on a bus in rural western Massachusetts, you are probably at the end of some sad story. Mostly you navigate the landscape, with its great, green interims of nobody and nothing, in your own car, on your own. The streets don't adhere to any comforting city-style grid. They curve and search passage through the countryside. Their names change when you cross the town line just in case, for a brief moment, you **weren't** lost or confused. They lead to strange places.

Sometimes Jonathan Coulton would bring his family up to visit ours. Jonathan is a musician and my best friend. I hope he does not read that last part. I would never call him my "best friend" to his face. I am from Massachusetts and he is from Connecticut, and New Englanders do not say things like that. "Yankee ingenuity" means the canny improvised fixes, repairs, and craftwork our predecessors

employed to keep their barns and brains in-
tact through long winters without ever having
to break down and ask anyone else for help.
Shame, embarrassment, and crippling emotional reticence is what this part of our nation
was founded on, at least the white part, and
Jonathan and I adhere to this legacy.

One summer when his family was visiting,
my wife and Jonathan's wife, Christine, had
taken our children somewhere else for the
day—probably to go look at some emus—
and Jonathan and I had the afternoon to
ourselves.

"It is very hot," Jonathan said, and that was
true. "Is there any place around here to go
swimming?"

I told him yes there was. A few miles away
from our house the shallow, burbling termi-
nus of the North River surrenders to the deep,
cold Deerfield River to form a swimming
hole the locals call Sunburn Beach. It has a
shoreline of smooth, flat boulders you can
sit on with round "potholes" in them, carved
out by centuries of grinding river water and
small stones. It is a great place to swim, I told
Jonathan. You can wade around in the warm

shallow part or jump off a high overhang into the deep part. I know you can do this because I have seen the locals doing it as I have driven by on the road that is sometimes Route 112 and sometimes Main Street. I drive by, but never stop.

"Let's go," said Jonathan. As if you could just **do** a thing like that: drive to a semi-legal swimming hole that you have to cross unclear property lines to reach and just swim there, among the year-round residents, without any sort of invitation.

"Um," I said. "I don't know if that is allowed."

Jonathan said, "That's ridiculous."

So I took him to the river. We drove across the North River Bridge to the little incline where all the locals park: right on the side of the town road, right underneath the town signs that say "NO PARKING." Then we walked across the street to the wooded embankment where every year Franklin County erects a small fence to bar the locals from walking the well-trod path down to the river, and every year the locals stamp it down. I stepped over this stamped-down fence. The whole experience was nauseating. But I am a gracious host, and Jonathan, after all, is my pretty good acquaintance.

We walked down to the river's edge. The scene there was exactly as I described (I am good at describing stuff), and we took off our shirts (disgusting) and went swimming.

And do you know what? Swimming is fun. It is easy to forget that swimming is fun because it first requires the denuding of your gross and shameful body and, in this case, walking through a bunch of mud and sticks and riverbank ants before you are there, deep in the middle of the river, weightless, embraced and cloaked in dark water, swimming cold against the current.

We did this for a while and we had a good time. And then we took a break to walk around the shallows. Jonathan tapped me on my shoulder (my **bare** shoulder; disgusting), and he pointed and said, "What are those?"

"Ah," I said. "Those are the cairns."

If you don't know what a cairn is, I am here to tell you. A cairn is a small, artful pile of stones that you see around in nature from time to time. They are a kind of folk art.

Often hikers will build them as messages to other hikers yet to come. A little cairn will stand there at a branch in the trail as if to say, "Go this way for beautiful hiking!" Or "Do not go this way because of bear nesting." It's not clear what, really, the cairns are trying to say. And also "bear nesting" is not a thing. The cairns are less helpful than they are spooky and quiet and never really on your side.

The cairns come every summer to the rivers of rural western Massachusetts: spindly towers of smooth river stones, carefully balanced one by one, rising out of the shallow bed and a foot or two above the waterline. That's what Jonathan saw now: dozens and dozens of cairns, all standing mute sentry in the North River shallows, going back at least a half mile. That's why he touched by bare shoulder.

I explained to him that when it rains, the cairns will wash away. And then a day or two later, they will be back again.

"Who makes them?" asked Jonathan.

"Nobody knows," I said, meaning at least one person does not know, and that person is me. "It's probably the Dumpmen and their people," I said, "or maybe witches."

My assessment was reasonable. There definitely are witches about. At the turn of the twentieth century, spiritualists and psychics clustered tiny gingerbread cottages around Lake Pleasant in Montague for summertime séances and spirit healing. Eventually factions grew out of a dispute over reincarnation. Followers of George Tabor Thompson, known as the Psychic Songster, believed in reincarnation. The faction that didn't ended up dying out, never to come back. Thompson Temple, however, survives, even after a devastating fire destroyed much of the community. Both sides proved their point.

Later the hills were populated by '70s-era back-to-the-landers. They went into the woods to practice a life in tune with nature. Some went a little too deep, and you stumble across their houses if you nose down the wrong rutted path: big old Victorian painted ladies with lawns full of pyramids and gargoyles, god's-eyes and mirrored spheres. How many of them are attempting actual magicks I could not say. But if you're going to take the time to put a crystal ball in your birdbath, you probably also will stack stones in the river at night, probably while nude.

Western Massachusetts, like all of Massachusetts, is perceived as a liberal Utopia: good witchin' country. But it is still the country. There's a reason Bernie Sanders opposed new gun regulation, because his Vermont hills, like ours, are home to an equal population of hunters and truck owners and Trump voters. You see them by the rivers too, perched midstream on lawn chairs, galvanized buckets of beer chilling in the eddies at their feet, daring you with big smiles to ask them to turn down the country music station on their jobsite boom boxes. They have a good time. And it would be the height of my own citified arrogance to suggest that there is no way they could be building these cairns.

I explained this social landscape to Jonathan, and he agreed that it was very interesting and that my insight into my neighbors wasn't condescending or reductive at all. But when he suggested that we, he and I, go and make some cairns ourselves, I took my stand.

"Um," I said. "I don't know what the rules

are about that." I told him I was honestly not sure if it was legal for a human being to put a rock on top of another rock. And in any case, whoever is making those cairns clearly has a plan in mind, like summoning a river nymph or spelling out "MAGA." I didn't want to knock over one and trip a silent cairn alarm and end up in Dump Jail like my old man.

But Jonathan said, "That's ridiculous." And so we did it. We went out to the middle of the shallow water, and we cairned.

It was a transforming experience. You know how I'm pretty good at everything, usually on the first try? That's documented. Talk to my old clarinet teacher. Well, in this case I must confess to you that my first cairns were ass. I was grabbing rocks from all different geological strata, smashing dark granites in with bone-white quartzes. Amateur hour.

Naturally, I went for the big rocks, the showy ones with flashy colors and boss marbling. I hauled them out of the mud as if strength mattered even for a second in cairn building and used them as the base for huge, high monuments to overthink: towers that split in two to become double towers, and then triple towers. And then I would step back and see how terrible they were. My cairns were obvious, pretentious, rococo. They looked like the tacky resin lawn fountains you used to be able to buy in the garden section of the late/lamented SkyMall catalog. (I miss you, SkyMall. See you in heaven or hell soon.)

But Jonathan. Jonathan is a musician, but he also has the soul of an engineer, and you could see it in his cairning. He understood it right away: matching like-colors with like-colors, like-shapes with like-shapes, into delicate, less-is-more spindles of round, smooth, darkly onyx stones, each a little smaller than the last and culminating with an almost microscopic pebble. Then he moved on to advanced maneuvers: a near perfectly round offering of granite, about the size of an emu egg, sun-warmed and ancient, perched upon a miniature Stonehenge. He balanced huge stones impossibly on top of small stones. He created arches and buttresses. I swear I saw him float a stone in the air. He was over there making Yes album covers, and here I was, with my gaudy Trump Towers of rock junk.

I never wanted to kick my pretty good

friend in the cairns so bad. But in a moment of rare self-editing, I didn't. I kicked my own cairns down. I started over, and learned from my mistakes. I sought stones more patiently, I stacked more delicately, letting each stone lead to the next: click, click, click.

We did this for hours. We disappeared from each other, and then the afternoon disappeared behind us. Rain came, and we didn't look up: click, click, click. And then it stopped, and the sun warmed our bare backs as we moved from cairn to cairn, adding stone after stone, click, click, click. Click, click, click. Click, click, click. Click, click, click. Click, click, click. Click, click, click. Click, click, click. Click, click, click. Click, click, click. Click, click, click. Click, click, click. Click, click, click. Click, click, click. Click, click, click.

Oh, I forgot to mention: we were high out of our minds.

I apologize. That is important context to this story that I left out. Let me clarify: earlier in the day, when our wives went out with our children and Jonathan suggested we go swimming, **first** he said, "I have marijuana," and I said, "Yes." So we each took an edible when we reached the river, and now here I was, on the lingering end of a half-legal high, half-clothed, half-submerged in a river equidistant from either shore, reveling in ambiguity, half-literally half-**bathed** in ambiguity, just a human putting rocks on top of other rocks.

Eventually the sun got golden and low, our edible spell broke, and it was time to go home. We walked up the bank and this time I didn't qualm while I stepped over the fence. I may have even stamped it. I can't remember because it was probably a small half stamp, a respectful stampette. I walked up the road, right on the yellow double line, until we reached my car, standing alone and unmolested in its no parking zone. Everyone else had long gone home. It had been a good afternoon.

I was in the midst of thanking Jonathan for suggesting swimming and setting me on a new life path when I saw it: a Honda Civic, crossing the North River Bridge. I am not a car person, but thanks to the year-by-year mug book that is the Wikipedia Honda Civic page, I can testify that it was probably a third generation hatchback, 1986-ish. It was making for us, fast, with more searing menace than you typically get from a Civic. It was pale blue, with a rusted panel on the front right corner and tinted windows. There were no markings or bumper stickers that might reveal whether it was the Dumpmen or the witches, but I felt immediate, gut fear. I felt fear when the Civic was driving fast, and I felt more fear when it stopped going fast and started a slow, police-style roll past us, passenger or passengers invisible behind dark windows. **Who**, I thought, **tints the windows of a Civic?**

But before panic could set in, they passed us, speeding up again and around the curve, gone forever. I restarted my breath with a choke-laugh. Ha ha! Ambiguity! I was just explaining to Jonathan that I was afraid that Honda Civic was the cairn police and how ridiculous I was, and Jonathan was agreeing, when **IT CAME BACK.**

The Civic had gone around the corner, and after one long, horror-movie beat, it nosed back around again. It headed straight for us, and then it stopped. I looked at Jonathan. Even he was confused now, and scared. This was **not** ridiculous. We were alone on a country road with an idling Honda Civic of unknown intention. Whoever was inside the car began to crank down the windows. That's right: crank. That's the kind of people we were dealing with.

It was neither Dumpmen nor witches. It was children. Well, "children" in contrast to me. There are a great number of colleges and universities just south of where we now stood. And so the region is flooded with young people. You see them in Northampton and Amherst, glowing and gliding around on the belief that their feelings are unique and that they will never regret their full arm and neck tattoos because their skin will never age and their tastes will never change. You sometimes see them up here in the hills, and even down by the rivers, lying on the rocks, airing out their loathsome Caucasian dreadlocks and testing their new theories of public nudity. And here were three of them: a young man behind the wheel, and two young women, staring out at us, two older men who were quickly realizing they were not going to die today.

The young man opened and closed his eyes. "Excuse me," he said. "Are you Jonathan Coulton and John Hodgman?"

"Well," I said. "The billing is **usually** John Hodgman **with** Jonathan Coulton. But the answer is, yes."

"I knew it!" said the young man. "I tried to tell them," he said, meaning the young women, "but they didn't know who you were."

"That is fairly typical," I said.

"Hi," said one of the young women. She never spoke again.

"Jonathan Coulton!" said the young man. "I am such a fan of all your songs. The story of how you gave up your job as a computer programmer just as you and your wife were having a baby and followed your passion, recording your own songs about zombies and robots with feelings and putting them on the internet on a pay-what-you-can basis and cultivating a devoted fan base and a new career for yourself as a completely independent artist is really inspiring to me!"

"And John Hodgman!" he said, turning to me. "You are still on television sometimes."

"Thank you," I said.

This dialogue is all accurate, by the way. I remember it perfectly.

"What are you guys doing here, in rural

western Massachusetts, in the middle of the road, with your shirts off?"

Now, after this afternoon's awakening, I was a little offended. "Come on," I said. "You know **me**. I was down in the river, getting high and making cairns. That's what my life is all about now."

"Really?" said the young man. "That's cool!"

"Yes," I said. "We **are** cool. We are in our forties and we are **really** cool."

"OK," said the young man. The young woman next to him put her hand on his arm: time to go.

"Hang on," I said. "I have an idea," and I **really** did.

I took Jonathan aside and I said, "Jonathan, do you still have any of that edible marijuana?"

Jonathan said he did, and then clearly regretted saying that.

"Perfect," I said. "Here is my idea. **Let's get these kids high.**"

"No," said Jonathan.

"They are our biggest fans. It's going to blow their minds to get high with their cool heroes."

"No thank you," said Jonathan.

"Yes. Let's get them high. And **then** let's get into their car and let them drive us wherever they want!" I explained to him that this would be exciting and youthful and unpredictable! Just like riding a bus!

This did not end up happening. Jonathan took the car keys away from me. We said good-bye to our new friends, who seemed happy to leave. I do not know where they went in their lives after that, but I have learned to be comfortable with that. Jonathan and I went back to the house. We probably watched a movie or worked on a puzzle. I don't remember. It was nice to be home.

That night, Jonathan was taken by witches. He should have listened to me. I miss my friend.

Pills Are Science

Obviously, Jonathan Coulton was not taken by witches and replaced with a duplicate Jonathan Coulton, a bearded, pop-folky golem made of cursed wax and twine. He is just fine.

But I was not lying about the marijuana, and now I feel I owe some explanation to my children, who may be reading this. Children, here is the truth: I like marijuana. Not often. And never when you are around. I am a grown-up; I like marijuana pills; and from time to time I eat them.

I appreciate that this conversation is awkward. I remember when my mom made her own marijuana confession, and she didn't have the decency to write it in a book so that I could just quickly close it and walk away. She cornered me in a hotel room in the mid-afternoon. I was about twenty-one, I suppose, and we were all on a trip to Seattle. There was some professional reason for this, a nursing conference or something. But that was an excuse. They would bribe me with a plane or train ticket and I would take it because (a) Seattle in the early '90s! And (b) I loved them and (c) I was growing up, and we all knew we would not be taking family trips like this for much longer.

So maybe that is why she seized this moment to say, "I tried marijuana a couple of times in college. I didn't like it."

I don't recall if I believed her story or not. I was concentrating too hard on staring into the middle distance, waiting until it would be acceptable for me to leave the hotel as planned on my own and drink some beer and listen to some grunge-rock music. There are few things I dislike more than beer and rock clubs, but you have to understand I was experimenting at that time. It's embarrassing and I apologize.

I also don't recall if I told her the truth when she asked if **I** had ever tried marijuana. I had, just once, and not that long before.

The first time I had marijuana was in the South End of Boston with Michael and Kenny. Kenny was a projectionist at the Coolidge Corner Theater where I had worked summers and vacations. He was tall and quiet and wore fedoras and was gay. He had a Doberman pinscher with a girl's name that I am ashamed to say I have forgotten. Let's call her Alice.

The group at the Coolidge was a mix of young people like me and an older crowd, mostly artists, for whom it was a night job. I had become very close friends with some people at the Coolidge, but Kenny was not one of them. He was shy. Michael, the man who today would be Kenny's husband, often kept Kenny company at Coolidge and was his bright and loquacious conduit to the world. One day, Kenny showed up with an eye patch. He had gone blind in one eye because, we all soon learned, he was dying of AIDS. Alice, meanwhile, was dying of sadness.

Kenny got worse and stopped coming to work. Around this time Michael invited me to lunch at their house on a Saturday afternoon, one of a series of good-bye lunches he was arranging. And even though I didn't know them well and no part of me wanted to do this, I knew that you cannot say no to such an invitation. And now, children, you know this too.

They lived in three tiny rooms in the South End. I don't remember much of lunch other than that the food was good and Michael was funny and Alice was sad and Kenny was quiet and brave and his eye patch looked amazing. Small comforts. After lunch we went from one tiny room to another, and Michael drew the blinds and asked, "Would you be interested in smoking some pot?" Which is slang for marijuana.

I was honestly not interested, and Michael seemed prepared to accept that answer, even to anticipate it. But then he mentioned that he had the same marijuana source as the Kennedy family. Well, look. I enjoy the finer things. And I wasn't going to turn down the chance to be a part of history. So I smoked.

By this time I probably had already begun smoking cigarettes. I have asthma, and cigarettes would eventually kill my mother, who could not have been smarter or more unselfish in life except in this one very specific area. I inherited her dumbness regarding cigarettes for the same dumb reason many dumbs do: it feels good, once it stops feeling terrible. And plus no one is ever going to die, so why not?

But I also smoked cigarettes for another reason: they were legal.

I am not against drugs. I love drugs. I have taken them all my life. I have been sucking on a bronchial dilator since I was younger than you, children, along with an increasingly exotic array of inhaled steroids and antihistamines. Once I stole a handful of Vicodins from my friend's dorm room after he broke his leg, and I don't apologize for it. Because pills are **science.**

I like pills for the same reason that I prefer liquor to wine. Gin and whiskey are chemistry, carefully formulated and distilled to create a single repeatable experiment in intoxication, the same precise flavor and effect across the brand, bottle after bottle, glass after glass.

Wine, on the other hand, is like religion: it's mysterious, sometimes literally opaque, and there are too many kinds of it. You never really know if a particular wine is good or bad; you just have to take it on faith from some judgy wine priest, an initiate to its mysteries. And wine is also like religion because the people who **really** get into it tend to be fucking unbearable.

But marijuana was worse. It was witch-craft, a dank and unpredictable weed pulled from the earth like screaming mandrake roots, delivered to your dorm room by some glassy-eyed druid with bad-smelling hair, and ritually burned in a brazier. More important: it was illegal everywhere and all the time back then, and, children, you know I was a good boy. I didn't even taste alcohol until I was eighteen, and then only in England, where the drinking age was eighteen. That's how far I was willing to go to follow the rules.

But now with Kenny and Michael and Alice, I smoked marijuana for the first time. We didn't talk much, and what I remember most was the sound of Alice's occasional long dog sighs, and around them that silence, getting warmer and softer. I felt the room fold and unfold around that silence. I was afraid to break it, because I didn't know what would come out of my mouth. And that was how we said good-bye: by not speaking, in a room that contained cruelly three phenomena that would also soon pass on—two men unable to marry each other, AIDS as a certain death sentence, and adults hiding from their neighbors behind closed blinds as they take quiet, sad communion in each other over their Kennedy-grade chronic.

So yes, children: if you are offered to share comfort in marijuana with a dying man and the man and dog who love him, I will support that decision. If you are offered marijuana at a party by a drummer, on the other hand, do not do it.

I never meaningfully tried marijuana again until I was forty-one. Then I began experimenting. Two reasons drove this decision. One, my metabolism was changing, and I figured that marijuana is probably less fattening than my nightly martini gallon. And two, as it has been legalized or decriminalized in various states and commonwealths, it has been regulated. The doses are state measured and chemically predictable. You can go into a shop in Seattle and a very nice man or woman with impressive tattoos will describe to you the very specific effects of each micro-strain. They will guide you through the world of innovation that legality has fostered: they are making marijuana into strips and tinctures and cookies and sodas and restorative soaking baths and things they call mints but we all know they are pills. The packaging for these items is well designed with contemporary typefaces without serifs or a single Grateful Dead dancing bear. And where once you would have been smoking marijuana out of a pipe shaped like a three-eyed wizard skull wearing a top hat, now you vaporize it in any one of a number of beautiful glowing iPhones. Once the new weed entrepreneurs essentially put marijuana into an asthma inhaler for me, who was I to say no?

But before you take this as a complete endorsement, children, please heed these fatherly warnings.

Your brains and bodies are working at peak power right now; give them time to do their thing. Don't undercut them with marijuana now. Wait until they begin to break down and betray you with knee pain and heel spurs and undefinable sadness. Then—YOU MAY GO FOR IT.

Wait! Don't go for it! First make sure you are not an addictive personality and are otherwise healthy, stable, and part of a functioning emotional support network.

And also that you are an adult who has finished college and/or are established in a career you love. While I sort of love the fact that the tattooed smiling weed pharmacists of Seattle get to work legally and seemingly lucratively in a field they clearly love, DO NOT BECOME ONE.

And maybe wait till you're forty.

OK? Good. Now GO FOR MARIJUANA.

But wait, my forty-year-old children! Before you begin your own experimentation, listen to my chilling true story. It follows.

Daddy Pitchfork

A couple of years ago, when I was truly in the prime of my midlife marijuana research, I was invited to speak at a college. It happens from time to time that colleges invite me to stand in a gym or a multipurpose room at the campus center and perform my imitation of stand-up comedy for students who are inevitably half-listening while wearing their pajamas. I enjoy doing this. I like sharing my life wisdom with young people. And usually on college campuses, unlike most American cities, you can get food after the show. There is usually one diner or sub shop or food truck open very late where I can get an extremely ill-advised steak bomb or scrapple, egg, and cheese hoagie with hash browns in it that I can eat by myself in my hotel room while watching reruns of **Friends** dubbed in French, if the college is near the Canadian border. That happened once. It was a worldly experience.

I was especially excited to speak at this college, though, because my appearance was scheduled for 4/20, a marijuana-specific date that **I know about**. And because college is where marijuana lives, and because Jonathan Coulton was nowhere nearby to stop me from making really good decisions about my life, I predicted that those kids would love me and give me marijuana.

I will not reveal the name of this particular college. I will only say that it is a lovely, small liberal arts college in the northern part of the American South. I had been asked to give the school's annual Samuel Clemens Address. Now as you know, I am striving to be more candid and vulnerable in my storytelling, so I feel that I can confess to you that I know very little about Mark Twain. I have never read **Huckleberry Finn** all the way through. I have never read **Tom Sawyer** at all. In eighth grade we read **Pudd'nhead Wilson**, the one about fingerprinting and race ambiguity. Then I went to an alternative high school and skipped most traditional American lit to read **One Hundred Years of Solitude** twice. This is a very embarrassing thing for an American humorist with a mustache to admit, but I am done lying to you.

The fullness of my Mark Twain knowledge

was that he had a big white mustache and wore a white suit, and that the actor Hal Holbrook made a career of impersonating him onstage. Here I felt a kinship, as this is the same as my own stage show, except I impersonate myself. I know that his real name was Samuel Clemens and that "Mark Twain" was an old steamboating term that a steamboatman would yell after measuring the river's depth. "Mark Twain" meant the boat had two fathoms of water beneath it, which is to say: safe for steamin'. I learned that fact when I was eight from a toy robot called 2XL that asked you trivia questions. As I type that, I realize that the many hours I spent alone on the floor of my room answering the trivia questions encoded on the eight-track tape you shoved into 2XL's belly still provide the core of my world knowledge today. 2XL was my Socrates.

I explained these deficits to the professor who invited me to give the lecture. To protect his privacy I will call him Mark Ta-ree, or "three fathoms of muddy depth!" as riverboating is apparently the best source for pseudonyms. He was a Twainologist, and so I felt especially nervous, but Professor Mark was reassuring. He said I had nothing to worry about. His department just had some money set aside for this annual Clemens Address, which he used to bring down comedians and writers he enjoys. I didn't have to say anything about Mark Twain at all. "Just come down and do some comedy and hang out," he said. Once I realized we were both opportunistic frauds, I felt much more comfortable.

I liked Professor Mark instantly, even though he liked me. He was about fifty years old at the time, not from the South but the American Southwest, and he was friendly in a way that a lot of white guys from those regions can be when meeting other white guys, which is to say **instantly** friendly and, to a person from New England, unnervingly so. He was there to greet me at the Campus Guest House, where I was to stay. I opened the door and Professor Mark was just there in the foyer. He smiled and said a big "Hey, buddy!" and I thought I was going to be murdered.

But he did not murder me: he showed me around the house. He showed me the living room and the screened-in porch overlooking the wandering, silvery river (fathoms unknown). He showed me the two bedrooms upstairs and then back down to the little kitchen with an array of Panera Bread sandwiches and a bottle of bourbon he had left in tribute. It was really nice. I said, "Is this really all for me?"

And he said, "Well, I was hoping I could change my clothes here," which is not something you expect or desire to hear from someone you have just met.

I said, "Right now?"

And Professor Mark said no, no, no. He explained that he lived forty minutes away. Rather than make the round trip home to change before the Clemens Address, he was hoping it would be OK for him to use the spare bedroom upstairs to change into his suit and tie.

"But don't worry," he said. "I won't be in your hair. I'm going to go take a walk and let you rest for a couple of hours. Then I'll take you over to the Address. So go ahead and feel free to shove all the chicken from those Panera Bread sandwiches in your mouth while pacing back and forth in a full-on, preshow calorie panic, and then wonder if I would notice if you drank half that bottle of bourbon before I came back to change clothes and bring you over to the show."

He did not say that, of course. There was no way he was going to know that that was exactly what I was going to do. I did eat all the chicken and threw away the bread, but I didn't drink the whiskey. Instead I went upstairs to fall into a Panera-induced, deep, dreamless nap, the cotton nubs of the white bedspread digging deep into my cheek. Then I woke up and got dressed in my three-piece corduroy suit: a terrible outfit for even the north of the American South on a muggy spring evening, but it was the closest thing to Mark Twain cosplay I owned.

Professor Mark had come back while I slept, which is not as creepy as it sounds. Apparently he was changing into his nice clothes at the same time as I was, in the other bedroom down the hall. And when I opened my bedroom door, he opened his bedroom door at the exact same moment, and there we were in our best suits, facing each other across the

little landing. I thought it was like the opening of a sitcom, or a heist movie about two
guys planning to rob a small liberal arts college. But Professor Mark nailed it. "Look at
us," he said. "We look like two brothers going
to a wedding."

"That is a **good** line," I said. "I guess that is
why you are an expert Twainologist."

We walked across campus together, two
brothers in their suits in the golden glow of
a northern southern twilight. It was a beautiful campus, less manicured than most, full
of lush lawns rambling down to the river,
crossed with slithery paths of tarmac upon
which beautiful young people floated by on
their strong, jogging legs or various iterations
of wheels. They all greeted the professor, and
he greeted them, one by one: "Hello, Cody.
Hello, Paige. Hello, Trip." (Those were their
names.)

One by one he would ask them, "Are you
coming to the Clemens Address tonight?"

And one by one they would smile and say,
"Nope!"

Young people are such natural sociopaths.
They could have lied and said, "Yes." Pro-

fessor Mark would never have noticed their absence when they didn't show up. But why should they bother? Why lie to spare the non-feelings of this faceless older mannequin who makes mouth noises about Mark Twain to them twice a week? They were asked a question, and so they gave an honest answer: nope!

Cody in particular was taken aback by the question, and answered it only with a face full of guileless confusion.

What? his face seemed to say.

What did you ask? Am I going to the Samuel Clemens Address tonight? Well, let me think. Even if I had bothered to remember this thing you've been talking about in class for weeks (which you have to admit, professor, is a pretty unreasonable expectation), even then the answer would probably be: no.

Because this is Saturday! And may I remind you, professor, it is also 4/20. So as for tonight, I hadn't really thought it through, but I think I'll probably smoke marijuana. In fact, now that I say it out loud, I'm going to make it a plan. I'm going to smoke a little, and drink a little, and maybe

go to a party. I've heard Paige is having a naked party tonight. (That is something we young people do because we all look good naked and are too young to give a shit about our furniture.) And after that naked party I'll probably go out and eat two or three whole pizzas, or a steak bomb. But rather than going sadly back to my room to watch Friends reruns, I will instead go back to the party. And surprisingly I will be thinner and better looking than when I left, because I have the metabolism of a white-hot sun.

Then I'll probably have sex with a man or a woman—we don't really use labels anymore. And after that, I'm not really sure. I might just go back to my dorm room and watch a movie. Yeah. I'll probably just watch a nostalgic movie from my childhood. Because even though I am physically mature, inside I'm still very much a child who is terrified by the drunken, high, naked, fornicating adult I've become.

And so I'll probably bring out my blankie that I brought from home and still sleep with every night openly and without shame, because all of my roommates are going through the same thing. What's that? Which nostalgic movie from my childhood will I choose to watch? I'm not sure. Probably Harry Potter and the Goblet of Fire, because that came out in 2005. And in that year I was only ELEVEN YEARS OLD.

Oh sorry, I got distracted. What did you ask me? Will I go to the Samuel Clemens Address? I think you can understand that the answer to that is: nope, not ever. Ever ever ever ever.

His students' reactions made Professor Mark embarrassed for me. I was standing right there. He would say, "No, you guys, it's going to be cool. **John Hodgman** is giving the Address."

And then Paige or Trip or Cody would just look at me, a middle-aged man, standing there sweating in my three-piece fake Mark Twain suit. I would give them a little wave to say, "Change your mind yet?"

They didn't. I would get no marijuana from these children.

Before the lecture itself there was to be a

reception for faculty and big donors to the college over in the Old State House. Professor Mark told me that it was a perfect reconstruction of the original state house from 1676, erected upon the same site. This was the first I had heard of this Old State House party, but I said nothing.

Professor Mark wanted to drop his casual clothes in his car first. So we stopped in the Old State House parking lot, which I presume was not part of the historical reconstruction. It didn't look like a 1676 parking lot, more a 1989. As he was taking care of his car and wardrobe business, I noticed two men walking up to us.

They were two handsome, big white men with big white smiles. One was maybe fifty-five years old and the other was in his very early twenties. I knew they were father and son, because I had seen this in the American South before: prosperous fathers and sons hanging out together and dressing exactly the same. They were both dressed like dads: white roll-collar Brooks Brothers button-down shirts, no ties, chinos better than Dockers that still look like Dockers, loafers, blue blazers over their arms. They radiated contentment. The shriveled weirdo in me both recoiled from them and fluttered to their light.

Professor Mark emerged from the driver's side of his pale tan Saturn (specificity is the soul of narrative) and let out a bright, "Hey, buddies!"

He said, "John, this is [name forgotten for the rest of my life] and his son, [same]."

Professor Mark explained that he and the dad have known each other since childhood. That the dad had gone into some kind of lawyering or financing or businessman-type business nearby. He moved here, had a family, and now they hang out all the time again. Apologies if I don't remember every detail correctly, Professor Mark. I was not paying attention.

"He and I are best friends!" said Professor Mark.

Now you know my feelings about those words. So I wanted to say, "What? Are you twelve?" But because I am mostly only a monster on the inside, and what's more a **professional**, a performer who will not only give a Samuel Clemens Address for which he is unqualified, but also press the flesh at an Old State House wine mingle I never agreed to, I only said, "Nice to meet you."

It turned out that Dad and Son were **definitely** coming to the Samuel Clemens Address.

"Oh yeah, really looking forward to it," the dad or the son said. I don't remember because they were so similar.

Then the dad ducked his head and dropped his voice to conspiracy-meant-to-be-heard level. "Now, Mark. I wanted to say, I have a pretty nice bottle of single-batch bourbon I picked up on the way. Maybe after the lecture we can all go over to the Guest House and have a little party?"

Professor Mark said, "How does that sound to you, John?"

"Well," I said, "apparently I am your prisoner, so sure." I only actually said the last word.

And then the son said, "That sounds great, Dad. Also, I have some marijuana." He added, "Maybe after the lecture, we can smoke it."

He said this in front of three grown men,

one of whom was his **father**. I felt like I should start running.

But his father just smiled and said, "Four twenty, right, son?"

And his son said, "You know it, Daddy!"

There may have been fist bumps. I don't know because my vision had whited out briefly in shock. Obviously I had misjudged these two badly. Yes, they were both **dressed** like dads, but they were both **acting** like Paige, Trip, and Cody, and they were working HARD at it.

They were both deep into new music. At one point Dad spotted a CD in the pocket of Professor Mark's open car door and said, "Mark, is that the new **Taylor Swift album**?"

Professor Mark raised his palms. "I can't help it," he said. "I like it."

But the son came to Professor Mark's defense. "Don't apologize," he said. "That's a good album, Dad. But Professor Mark, have you gotten the new Tyler, the Creator yet?"

Professor Mark struggled to remember what his best friend's son was talking about. "No?" he said.

And then Dad said, "Oh, it's really good,

Mark. But, Son, I have to say, I like the new Earl Sweatshirt a **little** bit better."

And that was the way they were for the rest of the night, constantly talking about the bands they liked, going down increasingly obscure musical rabbit holes. It was humiliating. I had recently been doing a huge amount of internet work, studying the new songs that children like so I can remain young, vital, and relevant, but these two were just lapping me, trading trivia about bands with names like Deerloaf and Starfart and No Monster Club and Marc with a C and Nescafé Moments and Kooshbag and Loth. I'd never heard of **any** of those bands (even though I made up all but one of them).

When we went to the Old State House, I did my job. I chatted with young faculty members, a few of whom knew who I was and wanted pictures. I chatted with older folks who did not know at all who I was until I said, "I'm a PC," and we did pictures again. This sounds like I hate these things, but I love them. I am grateful for the attention. I love having words to say when older moms and dads ask me what I do, and I love hearing about their retirements and hobbies. Even as a grown-up, I love pretending to be a grown-up. And plus, the reconstruction of the Old State House was truly beautiful, with the big paneled doors open to the brick archways that framed the lawn and the river and the twilighting sky. And there were pigs in blankets.

But it turns out Dad and Son were too cool for an Old State House party. I didn't see them anywhere. After a while Professor Mark caught me to say it was time to start heading over to the Address. But he was worried: he couldn't find them. So I surrendered my plastic flute of cava to a side table and we went on a best friend hunt. We found them upstairs, in a low, long-paneled fake State House chamber, leaning out of the reconstruction of a window, smoking Parliaments and drinking Amstels and talking about Diplo or some garbage: Daddy Pitchfork and Pitchfork Jr.

Professor Mark said some words like, "Oh, come on, you guys"—annoyance clothed sheepishly in sadness and utter unsurprise. I saw something now, something that maybe

Professor Mark didn't even see: a story under the surface, and a gambit. Professor Mark was losing his best friend. Daddy Pitchfork had a **new** pal. He was buying bourbon to drink with his son now, not Professor Mark. And perhaps in unconscious answer, Professor Mark bought a different bottle of bourbon for me, a stranger and new buddy. "I thought I had come here to deliver a Samuel Clemens Address!" I wanted to say. "Not be a wedge in some dude's best friend love triangle."

Professor Mark, if you're reading this, I'll say maybe I'm wrong in my assessment of this situation. But probably not. I am very insightful.

Pitchforks **père** and **fils** apologized and dropped their cigarette butts into their Amstel bottles. We walked over to the college gym, and there I gave the Samuel Clemens Address, and do you know what? It was FINE. I just did my imitation of stand-up comedy, including a long bit of incredible improv surrounding the design of the state flag that hung from the gym ceiling. (I'm good at flag work.) True, the professor **did** trick me into whitewashing a fence about halfway through, but do you know what? Even that was fun, just like he promised.

(That is a reference to **Tom Sawyer**, of course. I just put that in there to show you I do know at least one other thing about the works of Mark Twain. There was no fence, but the metaphor stands.)

After the lecture, Professor Mark introduced a bluegrass trio he had invited to play. Again, nothing to do with Mark Twain. Professor Mark was just curating an enjoyable gym jamboree for his students and himself— an impulse I would applaud even if it hadn't been a great success.

The band was two men and a woman, I seem to recall, all young and glowing and tattooed playing old-timey songs. Professor Mark said to me, "You sing a little, right? Why don't you sing along with us to the next one?"

"No thank you," I said. But I stood onstage and listened. The song was "Rocky Top." "Rocky Top" is not a song of the South, nor of the north of the South, nor even of Professor Mark's Southwest, but of the hills of Appalachia. It's one of the seemingly thirty-five state songs of Tennessee. The Tennessee Volunteers use it as a football fight song, because it is fast and fun and tells a story of a remote paradise in the hill country. Rocky Top is a place without smog or smoke or telephone bills—the three conditions of Utopia. Once two strangers went up Rocky Top looking for a moonshine still, goes the tune, but the strangers never came back. It is fairly clear from context that they were murdered. It's a great song.

But while "Rocky Top" is very upbeat, at the end, I heard Professor Mark singing, and I appreciated how sad it is. It is really a song of lament for a lost place, a lost life. Even the song knows that the wish expressed in the very first line, to be back on Rocky Top, will never come true.

The last verse is especially sad. I listened to Professor Mark sing it:

**I've had years of cramped-up city life
Trapped like a duck in a pen.**

Now this is a terrible lyric. First of all "cramped-up" is gross sounding. And "trapped like a duck" sounds weird too. I admit that I'm a city boy myself, but you don't **trap** ducks, do you? You shoot them, right? I mean, maybe if you're banding ducks for scientific population studies, you **would** trap them first, and then release them. But somehow I don't think that's what a Tennessean dreaming of returning to idyllic mountain and moonshine life would be singing about. The point is, the metaphor raises more questions than it puts to bed. See? "Puts to bed." That's a good metaphor. You know exactly what it means. And I should know, as I studied LITERARY THEORY AT YALE.

(And with that line I am grateful that Felice and Boudleaux Bryant, who wrote the song, and the Osborne Brothers, who made it their signature song, are not here right now to knock my teeth in.)

But I had to give you that part of the lyric, because it leads to the transcendent final line:

> **All I know is it's a pity**
> **Life can't be simple again.**

I cannot fault the poetry of this line. It hit me hard and deep as I heard it in the gym. The song's message is no longer "I **wish** life could be simple again." It is not even "I **know** life cannot be simple again." It's "**All** I know." It is a consuming knowledge, an overwhelming sadness for what is lost that makes enjoyment of the present impossible.

Now normally I consider nostalgia to be a toxic impulse. It is the twinned, yearning delusion that (a) the past was better (it wasn't) and (b) it can be recaptured (it can't) that leads at best to bad art, movie versions of old TV shows, and sad dads watching Fox News. At worst it leads to revisionist, extremist politics, fundamentalist terrorism, and the victory—in Appalachia in particular—of a narcissist Manhattan cartoon maybe-millionaire and cramped-up city creep who, if he ever did go up to Rocky Top in real life, would never come down again.

But when I heard Professor Mark sing this line, I did not feel those things. I felt something else: a kinship. I felt a sudden sense of **friendship on the one hand** and **bestness**

on the other: two distinct concepts that I am not connecting in any way. But I felt them both.

After the singing, at the end of the night, Professor Mark quietly offered me thanks and what's more: reprieve. He said, "John, I know we worked you pretty hard today, and thank you. I know there was some talk about a party after, but please don't worry about that. You should just go on back to the Guest House by yourself if you like and get some rest."

I thought of him, driving home alone in his suit with his day clothes stuffed in the back of his Saturn.

"No," I said. "Let's go. We are totally going back to that little house and we are going to party. Get that kid and his father and everyone else you can find."

And so we went back across the lawns in the warm darkness and turned on all the lights at the Guest House. We had Daddy Pitchfork with us and Pitchfork Jr., plus some other younger faculty members and one guy wearing a vintage tuxedo jacket and chunky glasses (they are in every state of the Union now), and we did it. We forced a party.

Around the living room we had Professor Mark in the wing chair talking to a member of his department. Chunky Glasses was next to me on the couch talking to a young woman from the psychology department, and then over by the small table by the back screen door, Daddy Pitchfork broke out his bottle of bourbon and in a perfect Southern ritual poured one for his son first, then passed it around. To his credit, he also provided a bag of Chex Mix, which is a very gracious thing to do. Where I live in Park Slope we are not allowed to have such things. I dug around in the Chex Mix for the pumpernickel rounds. You put them into your mouth and they just begin to burn into your tongue, as they are steeped in Worcestershire sauce plus all the salt in the sea for a thousand years. I was beginning to like these guys.

I listened for a while as Dad and Son traded facts about Frank Ocean, and since I had taken bourbon and Chex Mix communion with them, I thought I would try to make friends. "What do you think about Macklemore?" I asked. Please note that this happened a few years ago. I had heard Sir Mix-A-Lot discussing Macklemore on a Seattle Public Radio show the previous spring, and then I looked up "Thrift Shop" on YouTube nine months later, so I was feeling pretty up-to-date.

"What about that cool song called 'Thrift Shop'?" I said.

Daddy Pitchfork quickly averted his eyes, ashamed for me. But Junior seemed legitimately confused. "Wait. Isn't that song from **last year**?"

And I said, "Probably. Yes? I don't know. Look: I am in my **forties** now. I do not know who I am or what I am supposed to be anymore. And I do not know when songs came out." But I do know, I did not say, that I do not like **you**.

At that point Chunky Glasses suggested maybe we should have some music, and should he get his speaker from his car? And I said absolutely yes. Because I was going to show them. He came back with a ridiculously huge powered amp that I could hook my phone into, and so I began to play my cool songs: Parquet Courts, Cloud Nothings, Destroyer.

The party started to come to life. To be

clear: nobody danced. We were all white, and these were all songs purposefully written for white people to not dance to. They were designed for brow knitting and almost imperceptible head nodding and trivia contests. And to my immense pleasure, that is what was happening.

Pitchfork Jr. elbowed his father. "Hear this, Dad? This is Purity Ring. I was just telling you about them. The producer and the singer live in different provinces of Canada and never saw each other when they were making this album."

Daddy Pitchfork cocked his head and let some Canadian electronica throb into his ears, and then nodded. "How about that?" he said. "They're pretty good!"

And I wanted to say: **Yes. They ARE good. And I am the one who knows this! I know this because, unlike your son, I saw them in Williamsburg** last year **because I know the guy who had just signed them. That guy used to be the drummer in a band called the Long Winters, but he grew up and got a day job and now runs a whole record label. I know** him **because I met the**

lead singer of the Long Winters at a benefit concert for Dave Eggers's nonprofit! It was the same benefit where I met David Byrne and St. Vincent BEFORE they met each other. I'm dialed in! I've made dinner for Black Francis and his family at the house that I OWN because we have kids the same age!

But I didn't need to say any of this. Because now they knew, and if you didn't know, now you know: no one has more cred than John Hodgman of Brookline, Massachusetts.

I just went on and played even **more** incredibly cool rap and indie-rock songs that I had heard about from NPR and McSweeney's: Jean Grae, A. C. Newman, Tune-Yards, the Mountain Goats, Thao and the Get Down Stay Down. People continued to not dance; it was a good party.

But then. I don't remember who it was that said it, probably Chunky Glasses or Pitchfork Jr. But someone said, "I just don't think Elvis Costello is very good."

Now this will make many people angry, but I do not care about Elvis Costello. As with Bob Dylan and Bruce Springsteen, I was born without a certain genetic pure-enjoyment receptor for Elvis Costello. I got the Tom Waits RNA instead. Many would have me murdered for this, but it's just a difference of brain chemistry, and it is my disorder to bear.

That said, I **appreciate** all those artists. I know that Elvis Costello is a brilliant songwriter and lyricist. I know that he is not merely good, but in fact, **very good**, and to say otherwise is not tolerable. Not at my Guest House Best Friend party.

So I went back to my phone and swiped through my library looking for that one Elvis Costello song I like to listen to. It was "Oliver's Army," and I played it loud.

I noticed then that Daddy Pitchfork stopped talking to his son. He looked up into some middle space and smiled. I did not notice then that Professor Mark did the same thing, at the same time. I do not think Daddy Pitchfork noticed this either, but at the same time they stood up. Then they saw each other and walked to my corner of the room, where I stood with my phone and my one Elvis Costello song. They knew this song. They put their arms around each other and sang it, knowing the words by heart, by friendship.

To my eye it was clear: Daddy Pitchfork wanted to be a friend to his son, who was growing so quick. And also he didn't want to get old and die. But when it came down to it, he was a grown man. And this grown man didn't want to be thinking about Purity Ring or memorizing the discography of Tame Impala. Part of him just wanted to be back on Rocky Top, singing the old songs, with his old friend. **And I made it happen.** I got the best friends back together again. And that's when I turned to Pitchfork Jr., preparing to say, "Check it out, son. I win. **I stole your dad!**"

But Pitchfork Jr. was gone. Somewhere in the middle of "Oliver's Army" he had gone outside, probably to smoke marijuana, maybe with the young woman from psychology, and definitely without me.

I never did end up having any marijuana that night. However, I did succeed at blacking out.

I drank many bourbons of both the Professor Mark and the Daddy Pitchfork vintages.

And then I woke up, and it was morning, and I didn't know where I was. I just shot up in bed, on top of the bedspread in what I did not remember was my bedroom at the Guest House. It was early morning. The window was open, and the sheer curtains floated on the cool spring breeze.

For a long time there was only that window and the scene it framed: a ribbon of bright blue sky shimmering above a ribbon of bright green forest; the ribbon of spring trees floating above a ribbon of bright blue river; and the river finally lapping up to a ribbon of bright green lawn. That combination of colors was all there was in the world, and all there was of me.

Gradually, I came back to myself. I slowly recalled the night before, and the dissolution of the party, and my good-byes and my trudge upstairs. Then I remembered other things, like my job and my name and the names of my wife and children. But that morning in the window was so vivid and otherworldly that I wondered if everything I remembered was in fact a dream. It seemed possible, then, that **nothing** I remembered was true. And when I stepped out of that bedroom door I would find a different life waiting for me. Maybe this was my own house, and not the Guest House. Maybe I would be younger or older. Maybe downstairs I would not find **my** wife and children, but a different family. Maybe I would no longer be an only child. Maybe I had a brother, and maybe we were going to a wedding.

And who knows? Maybe that is what happens **every** morning. Maybe we wake to a new life every day and grasp sadly at disappearing memories of the last one as we awaken, until they are finally burned off by the sun.

Obviously, I am not the first and far from the best to express these ideas. But I include them here for my children. I want to show them that you don't **have** to smoke marijuana to get deep and have sophomoric thoughts about the universe.

And of course, I was still me. Everything that happened that night had actually happened. I knew it for two reasons. One, I was still wearing my sweaty corduroy three-piece. And two, as I stood and smoothed myself for the journey home, back to my real family who had not disappeared (I am so lucky), I found something in my jacket pocket. It was something that had not been there before.

It was a CD-R (remember, this was the past). There were two words written in orange Sharpie on it: "Frank Ocean." And then there was a yellow Post-it: "John, check this out! Hope you like it." It was signed with the real first names of Daddy Pitchfork and his son. Had they handed it to me in person, there would be no need for that note. The conclusion was inescapable. They had written the Post-it and put the CD in my jacket as I slept.

So, children, please don't go to college and drink to the point of blacking out, even if you're in your forties. If the worst thing that happens to you is some dude plants a mix tape on your person, that is violation enough. And to Professor Mark and the Pitchforks, I hope I have not hurt you with these revelations. I had a great time, and I am your friend.

Nerve Food

We were in our early thirties when we took on our house in rural western Massachusetts. We were grown-ups, but only theoretically. When you live in New York or any big city, it is easy to fail at growing up. The city is designed to keep you in a state of perpetual adolescence. You never need to learn to drive if you don't want to. And even if you do drive you can go back to that bar you went to when you were twenty-one, and it will still be there, and it will still be called Molly's, and the older waitress there will still remember you and let you sit where you want. And five years later, when she is no longer there, when there is just a picture of her above the bar in a place of sad honor, and you know what that means and you don't want to think about it, guess what: you do not have to. Because no one is driving home, and you're back again, listening to "Fairytale of New York," which is still on every jukebox, falling into the same conversations you had with the same friends in the '90s: about how the internet is going to change culture, and what you are going to do when you grow up.

Or let's say later you move to Park Slope, Brooklyn, in your late thirties because you suddenly, impossibly, have some money coming in from television. You are able to actually buy an apartment, and you think, this is it: a mortgage, real estate taxes, a sleepy neighborhood full of strollers and unexciting restaurants. You have grown up. But it turns out all of Brooklyn is suddenly alive with a not-growing-up renaissance. You can walk for the first time to the newest bars to hear comedy and new music. You are surrounded by people younger than you whose sense of style is to look like you. Young men grow dad beards and cultivate pallor and belly chub. You are struck by how much the young barista's glasses look just like the ones your mom used to wear—square and huge, overwhelming her face—and double-struck by how much **Twin Peaks** trivia she seems to know. And you **know** that this is just fashion, that dressing like an old person is exactly what you used to do when you were a pretentious young person, but you bury that knowledge and enjoy the illusion: I am just like you!

And even if you **are** lucky enough to own your own apartment, it is not a freestanding house. It is still a glorified dorm. If something fails or breaks or clogs you do not need to fix it yourself; you call the superintendent or some other surrogate daddy to make it right. You do not need to shovel a driveway or clean a gutter. You certainly don't need to drive to the dump or know what a septic system is. I still don't **really** know what a septic system is, and technically, as of this writing, I own two of them.

A few years ago in rural western Massachusetts a sound started coming out of the woods. It was a low, repeating, guttural sound that I will perform for you if you meet me. It sounded like three honking calls from a dying swan—**HYUHH, HYUHH, HYUHH**—organic, but with almost a machinelike precision as it repeated itself.

HYUHH, HYUHH, HYUHH . . .
HYUHH, HYUHH, HYUHH . . .
HYUHH, HYUHH, HYUHH . . .

One evening, as we sat on the deck, bog-gazing, my wife turned to me and asked, "What do you think that sound is?" The sound had been going on for twenty-four hours a day for about five days, so her curiosity was piqued.

"I don't know," I said. "Tree frogs?" Which was not a terrible guess. By then I had learned enough of the country to say that frogs, tree and otherwise, make some crazy croaks, drones, chirrups, **skree-skr**ees, and **hyuhh**s and really do keep it up for a long time. If anything was going to sound like a dying robot swan, it would be a tree frog. But my guess was wrong. It was the sound of our sep-tic pump failing.

I should have known something was going wrong. In our basement, on the wall, is a box. This box contains the septic control panel. And on top of the panel there is a red dome light, like you find on top of an old police car. This light had turned on some days before and was now revolving, filling my basement with the pulsing scarlet light of EMERGENCY. It was not like I had not seen this light. I had gone down to the basement a couple of

times to use the dryer. I knew that it probably indicated bad things for our septic system. My solution was to stare at the light for
a minute or so, and then turn around and
go back upstairs. My experience with com-
puters had taught me to trust that a spinning
red alert light is probably all part of the process. If I turn it off and on again, or just leave
it alone, it will probably fix itself.

It did not fix itself, and so we had to call
the Septic Daddy. It was an expensive lesson, but that doesn't mean I learned it. Even
now my brain refused to absorb the explanation for what had happened, or the solution.
It involved the relocation of the leach field, I
think. But then I may only remember that because I enjoy the term "leach field" so much.

To be fair, we treated that septic system
badly. The house came with a garbage disposal, which was exotic technology to us at
the time. We had both had them as kids, but
when we moved to New York they exited our
lives. You were not allowed to have a garbage
disposal in Manhattan then; the sewer pipes
were too delicate. But now, with a disposal of
our very own, it seemed a direct link to the

kind of easy suburban lifestyle we thought might never be ours. So it is fair to say we went a little disposal crazy.

Our first summer there my wife discovered a cache of old pantry items my mother had hoarded and left behind. Can after can of beans and soup and olives that were all now past their due date. "What is all this stuff?" she asked me.

I didn't know. It was upsetting. I do not know why my mother had bought all these cans of food, never to open them. When you get a can of soup, the date printed on the bottom is a distant future, impossible to reach. To hold a can of tomato soup now, two full years **past** that date, was like holding betrayal. **You were supposed to last forever**, I wanted to tell it.

My wife wanted to lay claim to this house and clear all this dead food out, and her plan was to disposal every last bit of it. She started opening and grinding, opening and grinding: cans of Stewart's shelled beans and jars of old pickles and capers. It went on for hours. It was a hot Saturday summer afternoon. I sat at the kitchen table, watching her sweat and open and grind. It was probably the most erotic moment of our marriage.

Eventually she found her way to the back of the cupboard. She dislodged three boxes of Cheerios, yellow and blue. They were five years old. She showed them to me.

"What are you going to do with that, baby?" I said.

"I'm going to disposal **all** of this," she said.

"That's fucking right you are," I said.

She did. It was a terrible idea. Here is some homeowner's advice. Do not put even a **single** box of stale Cheerios down the garbage disposal, never mind three. Because when you grind up Cheerios into oat powder and shove them into your pipes with a bunch of water behind them, the Cheerios do not slide easily through your pipes to the leach field (maybe?). They absorb the water and swell up. And then you have a Cheerio tumor in your pipes. And then you have to explain that tumor to the plumber you have had to call to cut it out. He will stand in the basement with his hacksaw, tapping at the Cheerio metastasis, the pipe making a solid, grim **thunk**.

He will look at you and say, "How did this happen?"

And you will have to say, "I'm sorry, Pipe Daddy. We were just having a sexy disposal time."

Here is another bit of homeowner's advice. If you have never owned a freestanding house that is heated by propane, you may not know that the propane does not arrive by magic. This came as a great surprise to me. If you had asked me that first year we spent in rural western Massachusetts where the propane came from, my best guess would have been: "Um, tubes of some kind?" And beyond that, who knew?

I didn't know what that giant white metal Tylenol out in the backyard was for. I thought it was just some weird personal submarine my father had collected. But that is not what it is: it is a propane tank. If you want it to be full of propane, you have to call the Gas Daddy. And if you do not call him, the Gas Daddy will not come.

And that is when you arrive at your home in rural western Massachusetts in November. You will have a baby in your arms, and it will be late at night, because you had to stop twice along the way to feed that baby. Your house will be cold and smell of garbage. This will not be because of the five bags of rotting garbage you left in the garage the last time you were here, two months ago. No, the Gas Daddy will explain when he arrives that night to fill your tank: the propane itself is purposefully made to smell like rotting garbage. That way, if you have a gas leak, you will smell it. Or, if you are running out of propane and it won't light anymore, you will smell it and call to get more. That smell is the propane's way of telling you that you have an emergency, he said. It smells like garbage because **you** are garbage: garbage people who do not deserve to own a home. We got better at it, but it took a while.

Unlike the city, where you are surrounded on all sides by humanity's tributes to its own false triumphs (condominiums and Whole Foods), the structures you build in the country do not protect you from all those things in the woods: the tree frogs, yes, but also the ants and the mice that will find their way in, and the wasps that will nest in your eaves

and attack your baby for their own sick fun.
Once a raccoon made a latrine of our porch.
That means it shat all over it. Why mince
words? A raccoon wouldn't.

Raccoons are beyond fear, and they are assholes. I tried to chase a raccoon off our porch
as it was casually emptying our bird feeder
into its fat mouth. As I yelled, it turned its
head and eyed me with such casual contempt
that I apologized to it. Once a raccoon used
its little mutant humanlike hands to open our
screen door while we were just sitting there,
gin-and-Scrabbling. It poked its head into
our human house and just looked at us sadly,
as if to say, "You guys know I could come in
here and kill you at any time, right?" I would
soon learn that the raccoon was telling the
truth.

This time, when we left our house for several weeks, a raccoon saw our porch and said,
"This is all mine now," and just started pooping. By the time we returned, the latrine was
a really developed and, I must confess, admirable heap of feces, both fresh and dried.
I was about to sweep it all away when some
reptilian survival impulse stopped me and

sent me to Google. It turns out that many raccoons are infected with a parasitic round-worm, **Baylisascaris procyonis.** By "many," I mean that it is estimated that some 72 to **100 PERCENT** of all raccoons have this worm inside them and are pooping out its eggs. If you were to accidentally inhale such eggs, say, by sending them into the air by sweeping a pile of old dry raccoon feces off your porch, they will hatch into larvae inside your body. In a few weeks you may begin to experience increasingly serious symptoms, which the CDC lists, with admirable comic deadpan, as "nausea, tiredness, liver enlargement, lack of coordination, lack of attention to people and surroundings, loss of muscle control, blind-ness, coma."

That quick trip from nausea to coma is for grown-ups only, by the way. If you are a baby and you get infected, you could die. That is why raccoons and wasps are such good friends: shared interests. The risk of infection is so serious that the CDC, a fed-eral agency, goes on to suggest that the best way to deal with raccoon feces on your porch is to attack it and your own property with a

propane torch. So call your Gas Daddy: nature is cruel, and it makes you cruel too.

It was in rural western Massachusetts that
I confronted that cruelty, and a profound
moral paradox. I was caring for a beloved
pet dwarf hamster during its end-of-life cycle.
If you have ever had a pet dwarf hamster,
then you know that its end-of-life cycle be-
gins about five days after you buy it for your
young son. That is when it suddenly stops
eating and starts becoming a hairless, half-
filled hacky sack of wheezes and ragged bones
that you are holding in your hand, hopelessly
trying to force-feed medicine from an eyedropper that was sold to you by a veterinarian/
con man for five hundred dollars.

This is what I was doing in our kitchen in
Massachusetts one evening: keeping one dwarf
hamster alive, while at the same time, just on
the other side of the kitchen door, in the dark
of the garage, I was murdering dozens of field
mice a week with traps and poison.

Now field mice are the exact same size as
dwarf hamsters. They are somewhat more
dusky in color, and somewhat more likely to
sneak in through the garage and live in the

walls and hide caches of seeds underneath your pillows if you are not around for a few weeks. But otherwise they are the same animal. The only difference is that this rodent, the one dying in my hand, is the one we chose to dignify with a name (Flurry!). This is the one we decided, arbitrarily, had value ($13.99, I think) and deserved love.

Even Flurry knew this was bogus. There she was in my hand, waving off the eyedropper of medicine with her withered paw, as if to say, "This is some insane cognitive dissonance. Please just let me die."

And I said, "No, Flurry. I won't give up on you. You are going to make it! Now you just rest quietly here for a moment while I go out to the garage to see how many of your brothers' heads I've smashed in today."

Because that is the humane way to kill mice that are invading your home: you quickly smash in their heads with a snap trap, rather than snaring them in a glue trap so that they can slowly starve to death. (Yes, you can catch them in a humane trap and return them to nature, where, having lived warmly in your walls for their whole lives, they can now revel freely in an exposed ditch somewhere until they are eaten by a hawk. Nature is the meanest trap of all.)

Every week, I would go out into the garage and collect the bodies, crushed in the spent traps, and throw them away. It never got easy. When you humanely crush a mouse's head in, their eyes bulge like dark blackberries full of shock and confusion. Their eyes seem to ask, **What happened? Why did it happen? And why did it happen to me, and not Flurry?**

There was no good answer as to why Flurry deserved to live. I mean, it's true that Flurry knew the term "cognitive dissonance." That's pretty impressive. But what it really came down to was that the dead creature in my hand was literally a country mouse, and Flurry was a city mouse. Tribalism is poisonous but powerful: I sided with the coastal elite.

Oh, but also, I would say to those sad and lifeless eyes, **Flurry never pooped one hundred times in my silverware drawer last night. So good-bye and good riddance, my eternal enemy!** And then I would throw the mouse body away and let it decay there, in the garbage bag, for months and months, unmourned.

Of course, we punished the mice to punish ourselves. We had lived with that mouse poop for a long time. For years we would come back to the house and open the drawer and once again see those little ice-cream sprinkles of mouse droppings in there, and say, "Oh well." We took out the silverware and washed the drawer. Eventually we surrendered to the mice, leaving the drawer empty for them and keeping all the forks and knives and spoons in upright glasses on the counter. When Jonathan and Christine would come to visit, we would say, "Oh, don't open those drawers, because they are full of mouse poop." And they thought that was a fine way to live. It amazes me that they would ever come back to our house—let's call it what it was, our shit house—but they did, because they were as young and as dumb as we were. None of us had children yet, so the full-feces immersion therapy that is caring for infants had not yet begun. If something seemed troublesome or gross in our lives, we would close the metaphoric drawer and walk away.

What was it that flipped the switch in our maturing brains to appropriate revulsion? I don't remember. One day I looked into the poop drawer, and the patterns the droppings made were like tea leaves, telling me a new and different story. **Right**, I remember thinking. **It is not OK to live this way. Grown-ups do not let mice poop in the drawer. Grown-ups do not let raccoons poop on their porch. The definition of a grown-up is that they deal with shit. That's almost all they do. They get shit done.**

That's when the traps came out.

We grew up in that house. But we didn't grow up **too much**. We didn't have to. For as I have mentioned, the region is full of young people and it has also been peculiarly attractive to rock musicians from the '90s. Indie guitarists and lead singers homesteaded in and around Northampton, Massachusetts, for a while, a small city and former home to Calvin Coolidge. I do not know what drew them there. Perhaps it was Northampton's very charming and passable imitation of a big city, with three-story brick buildings sheltering good coffee shops and record stores, theaters and concert venues, and a cool radio station. It has long-standing, overlapping communities of lesbians, activists, artists, writers, and glassblowers. One of my great regrets is missing the chance to meet Leonard Nimoy when he was in town for a reception at the art gallery that routinely deals in his beautiful photographs of nude people. You don't get failed chance encounters with Nimoy **and** nudes in a whole lot of rural America, so maybe that's why rock musicians picked this spot to do their own growing up and kid-having, in peace and quiet. Whatever the case, I won't violate their privacy by naming them here. Except one.

I met Black Francis near the petting zoo at a county fair. Black Francis is the lead singer of the Pixies. I had actually met him very briefly a few years before, as his wife, Violet Clark, had asked me to sign one of my books for her oldest son, who was then one of those strange and luminous thirteen-year-olds who are my key demo.

But the Heath Fair was the first time I had spent any real time with them and their family. When they moved to western Massachu-

setts I ran into them at a café, and we arranged
to meet at the fair: a weird, middle-aged full-
family first date. That is how I found myself by
the goat pen at the petting zoo, sitting down
at a picnic table, making small talk with one
of my cultural heroes. He was talking about
going back on tour. I was trying not to talk
about how important his work and his voice
had been to me, how the pure jangle scream
of the Pixies late in high school shocked me
into a new mode of being, one where I was
more tolerant of risk and adventure and less
inclined to listen to the mannered jump-
jive of Joe Jackson. Sorry, Joe Jackson. But I
couldn't actually say these things out loud to
Black Francis, who had introduced himself as
Charles. I think I admired the goats instead.
They were very good at jumping on top of
those little barrels.

I would not say that we clicked initially.
He is very decent and slyly funny. But he was
reticent. I suspect decades' worth of conversations with dudes who are pretending not to
freak out about the fact that they are talking to Black Francis will do that to you. But
I **could** joke and gossip easily with Violet,

who is also a very smart and talented musician but not someone I grew up with inside my head, and so I invited them back to dinner, and they said yes. This is the dinner I alluded to in a previous chapter. See? I was not lying!

The mouse poop stage of our lives was over at this point. There was nothing to be ashamed of in our drawers. I made vegan pizza for Violet's vegan son and talked to him about science fiction. The younger kids did their best to socialize. My own son suggested that he break the ice by blasting the vinyl copy of **Doolittle** that I had given him earlier as a primer on the subject of who was coming to dinner. I intercepted him just as he was about to drop the needle.

Violet and my wife were chatting at the table that had belonged to my grandmother, and Black Francis was mostly quiet until he opened the refrigerator to find dozens of cans of Diet Moxie. His face opened in a smile. He said, "I haven't had Moxie for years."

Moxie, if you don't know, is a very old regional soft drink native to New England. It was once known as Moxie Nerve Food, as its history goes back to the time when soda was patent medicine. Coca-Cola was served at the drugstore because it was a palatable delivery system for a healthy, natural stimulant called cocaine. Predating Coke, Moxie's own medicinal cred derived from a bitter slap of gentian root, giving it a flavor profile somewhere between Dr Pepper and witch hazel. It is difficult to enjoy even ironically, and so it has largely stayed within the confines of Massachusetts and Maine, where it is sometimes mixed with coffee brandy, as the people of Maine have a punishing streak of self-hatred that makes Bostonians seem like light-hearted imps.

I was explaining all of this to Black Francis as my wife shrugged (she's heard it all before). But I did not need to explain it to him because he is from Boston and knew most of it already. For the rest of the evening Black Francis depleted my Moxie cache can by can. The medicine did its work. We did not talk much more that night, but here was a line of connection, and for me a chance at some small repayment of an enormous debt. I have rarely been as happy.

I could pay this debt, and many other actual money debts, in part because I had just made a bunch of money. Obviously my life has always been privileged. My grandparents worked hard to foist their children up a rung on the class ladder (and also we benefitted from a nation's lifetime of policies, de jure and de facto, to help people who looked like us along).

I took all of this for granted. I stood lazily on all of these shoulders, and got so lazy I had forgotten to make any money of my own. I wrote for magazines and websites, and I was paid mostly in small checks and journalist swag. But you cannot support even a small family in Manhattan with a designer chef's knife, some mail-order beef jerky, a thorn-proof wax cotton jacket, or the fond memories of a junket to a Caribbean island where a man shot fine tequila into my mouth from a Super Soaker. I don't remember how high my credit card debt got as I continued to ignore this fact. Many tens of thousands. I became adept at averting my eyes from the total in shame as I paid the minimum month after month. Credit card companies loved me.

What my grandparents had done for my parents, what my parents had done for me, I would be unable to do for my own children. Now at the end of the long list of squandered advantages was this house in Massachusetts, my mother's house, which on many panicky 3 a.m. awakenings I would darkly fantasize about liquidating for cash.

But then I wrote a book, and then I went on television, and then I had money, real grown-up money. That sentence is as swift and dumbly easy as it all felt. And when it happened, all of those problems and all of that shame went away instantly.

This country is founded on some very noble ideals but also some very big lies. One is that everyone has a fair chance at success. Another is that rich people have to be smart and hardworking or else they wouldn't be rich. Another is that if you're not rich, don't worry about it, because rich people aren't really happy. I am the white male living proof that all of that is garbage. The vast degree to which my mental health improved once I had the smallest measure of economic security immediately unmasked this shameful fiction to me. Money cannot buy happiness, but it buys the conditions for happiness: time, occasional freedom from constant worry, a moment of breath to plan for the future, and the ability to be generous.

The motto of Massachusetts calls it "a quiet peace under liberty." To be in your own space, a space that is clean and free from mouse poop, and to have enough to share, to give vegan cheese and medicinal soft drinks to the people who have made your life better: that's the best version of being a grown-up. And I won't be shy about bragging about that night, or for violating Black Francis's privacy in the telling, because it made me appreciate how few get to enjoy this calm security, and what a crime that is.

I'm sorry, Charles and Violet. I enjoyed running into you both again when I performed at the Shea Theater in Montague, Massachusetts, last fall. I hope you are still enjoying rural western Massachusetts. I'm sorry we hardly ever go there anymore.

The Middle

~

Graveyard Fun

When my daughter was younger we would sometimes go to the cemetery. The cemetery is called Green-Wood. It is in Brooklyn, and its main entrance is on Twenty-Fourth Street where a giant, Gothic triple-spired gate presides. A colony of green monk parakeets, supposedly descendants of a long-ago pet store jailbreak, nest and chatter there among its cold, stony hollows. They liven up the cemetery. (Parakeets are famous ironists.)

But there is a side gate, nearer to where we live, that my daughter and I stumbled across one spring. It was just there at the end of Prospect Park West, hiding in plain sight after the last block of shops and houses and schools like a purloined letter. I was excited when we found it. I already loved our neighborhood, but to discover after years of living there that it also had a secret door to a massive Edward Gorey—esque necropolis was dreamlike, an embarrassment of weird riches. "Never forget what your father and mother have given you," I said to my daughter. "Let's go in."

I only had a mustache then. It was a rainy, humid, gray spring day and I was wearing a raincoat with my hood up and dark sunglasses for some reason. My daughter was wearing her red jacket and yellow boots. We approached the guard at the gate and he stopped us.

"Are you sure you want to go into the cemetery?" he said.

"Yes!" I said.

"I was not talking to you," he said. "I was talking to **her**." And then he looked at my daughter and said, "The cemetery is very large. There are many places you can go where no one could hear you if you needed help, even if there were a lot of visitors today, which there are not, because of the rain. So I ask again: are you sure you want to go into this cemetery, alone, with this man who has a mustache and is wearing dark glasses?"

"I am not afraid," said my daughter. "This is my father."

Reluctantly, the guard accepted this truth, and let us pass.

The guard was right. The cemetery was mostly empty, aboveground at least. But below, it was full to bursting. They don't bury many bodies anymore: they are almost out of room. So the ground was heaving with the dead, and nature feasted on it. We wandered over mounds of the greenest grass, and the limbs of the dog-woods, heavy with rain and fresh blooms, dipped to meet us as we navigated around the headstones and obelisks and peered through gated windows into dark tombs. It was vivid and beautiful and quiet and not scary.

In fact, I realized, **we** were the scariest thing there. There were a couple of actual mourners. They had the sense to drive through the cemetery rather than plod through the rain and muck. We ran into them from time to time on the road. Coming around a bend we would see their headlights and wave our hands in greeting, and each time, the car would slow and stop. I could not see into their windows, but I could imagine the inner debate as they paused.

Should we get out and save that little girl from that man?

Or should we flee from those obvious, terrifying ghosts who are creepily waving at us, luring us out of our car so that they can steal our souls forever?

After a while one impulse would win out over the other and they would drive on. It happened several times. It was fantastic.

"Let's come back here every Sunday," I said to my daughter. "We will stand by the side of the road and wave at passing cars. And as they turn on the road, we will run over the hill to end-run them and wave at them a second time, like that phantom hitchhiker from **The Twilight Zone**.

"Look at us. We have all the odd and specific details that make a good ghost story. People will say, 'I went to the cemetery and saw them! The pale girl in the red raincoat, and the mustache man who killed her.' They will tell the story to their friends, and soon enough people will come looking for us. They may even imagine they've seen us, even on those days we don't come. And even when you're in college and I am too sad to come here by myself, our journey through this underworld will become legend. We will continue, like descendants of descendants of the birds."

And that way, I told my daughter, we will live forever.

Part Two

~

Maine Humor

We hardly ever go to Massachusetts anymore because we have been spending more time in Maine. My wife grew up going there. Her grandmother had visited there for many years, and after her husband died, she moved there permanently. She bought a house in 1974 on a narrow peninsula that dangles south into a bay near Mount Desert Island. The sun touches Maine first among every state in the US. But Maine likes to confuse people and generally feels conflicted on the subject of light and warmth, so its shattered coastline of necks and points and isles hides from the sun, facing any direction but east.

The house was full of antique furniture and included a wide swath of land from one shore to the other, all costing something like a hundred dollars and a sack of shells. After many years, my wife's grandmother died. Her middle son lives in that house now year-round, a retired chemist and now full-time woodsplitter and family lore-keeper. Her youngest son is a semiretired boat- and housebuilder.

He built his own house and workshop with his own hands in a nearby town. He has lived year-round in Maine all his adult life. Her oldest son, my father-in-law, became a professor of English in Atlanta. But he is retired now too and lives half the year with my wife's stepmother in his own home by an interior, brooding private lake that suits their mood. The crags of Maine's landscape and culture offer few easy handholds. Altogether her family has been holding fast to both for half a century. None of them would be considered Mainers. They are still "from away."

Maine used to be part of Massachusetts, by some arrangement that made zero sense. They have never shared a border, and for most of the early life of the Union, Massachusetts ignored Maine, which was named either for a French province or a British town or for the fact that the dirt and rock portions of the state are not oceans, but the **main**land. No one knows for sure. Large parts of the region north of the Penobscot River were barely mapped, and essentially ceded to British Canada. It only became a state in 1820 as part of the Missouri Compromise. Missouri wanted to enter the Union as a slave state, so the US government needed to find a new territory to enter as a free state, because it was believed this would make the practice of owning other humans less brutally and eternally criminal somehow. It didn't. But in any case, the government was calling around to the states (and commonwealths) asking if anyone had any garbage land they didn't want, and Massachusetts said, "Oh yes! We **absolutely** do. We have this whole, massive hump of half-Canada up there that we never use. Take it." And that was how Maine was born: a new state, created in part to sustain a horrible evil, but only serving to delay its inevitable collapse by forty-three years— one further generation of legal slavery. Well, among white people. Considering the life span among slaves themselves, more like two generations.

To be fair, the humans of Maine did not seek this legacy. They just disliked Massachusetts and wanted to be alone. As they still do.

When you cross the Piscataqua River Bridge from New Hampshire's abbreviated, novelty coastline into Maine there is a sign at the border that says "MAINE," and beneath that, "VACATIONLAND." It also says "VACATIONLAND" on the license plates. This is either a cruel joke, or maybe simply an error. It may be that Maine is called Vacationland because when Maine was invented, we didn't really know what a "vacation" was yet.

After all, most humans did not take vacations until well into the twentieth century. If you lived in the country, you had a farm to tend. If you lived in the city, you had manglers to supervise or a shirtwaist factory to be burned to death in. The idea of having several days, never mind weeks or months, to relocate to a climate that was better for your lungs or gout, or to have an extra home in which to practice bridge strategies and indolence, was unimaginable to all but the most wealthy Bostonians, who were inbred and warped. Their idea of vacation was to go north, to a cold dark place, where they would not speak to their families but instead sit in silence, drinking martinis, looking out over bodies of water that you would never, EVER go into. Because the waters of Maine are made of hate and want to kill you.

The ocean in Maine is traumatically cold. If you make the mistake of going into it, every cell in your body will begin shouting the first half of the word "hypothermia" into your brain; the second half will simply be frozen tears. And the beaches of Maine offer no relief as you launch yourself back onto shore, because the beaches of Maine are made out of jagged stones shaped like knives. Wherever the shoreline is merely slopes of smooth, unpunishing granite, Maine compensates by encrusting it with sharp barnacles and sea snails. No matter how careful you are, you cannot avoid crushing some of them under your feet. You become death when you walk on a beach in Maine, and every step is a sea snail genocide.

To be fair, there are also lakes in Maine. But you do not want to swim in them either, because lakes are disgusting. At least the ocean has tides, heaving its weeds and slimes and jellies out of your way every now and then. The ocean takes its garbage to the dump.

But lakes are unmoving, fetid pools full of fish poop and frog parts. I don't want to hear from you people who live in the Great Lakes regions. I am sure you will protest that your gigantic stale-water ponds **also** have tides and are basically imitation seas. That is even weirder. That's like a dog pretending to be a human. And because it's a stupid dog, it just wears a rubber human suit and everyone says: **Why is that gross rubbery human crawling around on the floor over there?**

And the bottom of every lake is a Lovecraftian hellscape. If you ever go snorkeling in your father-in-law's lake in Maine, you will see for yourself that it is all ooze and muck and fallen trees and sunken demonic cities of impossible geometries. That last part is not true, but this is: you will see huge freshwater clams, and you will scream underwater. You will run through the foot-swallowing mud of the shallows and shore and back up to the house to seek confirmation of the madness that had just invaded your eyes.

And your father-in-law will say, "Yes: freshwater clams. They exist."

Indeed, "They Exist" would be a pretty

good slogan for a line of canned freshwater clams. But such a line will never exist. No person or thing wants to eat a freshwater clam, because all they do is suck in tepid fecal water all day. And, lacking natural predators, the freshwater clams grow to the size of Nerf footballs. They sit half-submerged in the mire, their pale shells opening and closing, singing to you as you snorkel above, "Join us, join us, join us."

You don't tell your father-in-law about the singing.

And even though scientists have done research and human explorers have, over the past one hundred years, discovered bodies of water that are actually appealing to enter and beaches that are not painful but in fact soft and warm and welcoming, the fact remains that **people are still choosing to go to Maine**, including us.

Because my wife loves Maine more than any other place on Earth, and because she also loves Maine more than any other person on Earth, we have visited Maine for some stretch of time almost every year that I have known her. Even when we grew up and had a per-

fectly good bogside summer home of our
own in Massachusetts, we would abandon it
every summer and begin the seven-hour drive
northeast to her father's house.

We would drive up along the coast, always
stopping at the same place where she stopped
as a child: Perry's Nut House. It opened in
1927 in a former ship captain's home: two stories of white shingles and green shutters now
looming anachronistic and lonely next to the
gas stations and failed restaurants that sur-
round it on Route 1 outside of Belfast. Perry's
Nut House did not begin life, as I first imag-
ined, as an old-time roadside lunatic asylum.
Rather, it began and still serves as a tourist
trap: a place for those wealthy Bostonians of
yore to rest the engines of their Model As and
Studebaker Dictators (thanks, Wikipedia!)
on their way to Bar Harbor and stock up on
bridge mix and nuts. Remember, they were
still inventing "vacation" back in 1927. Someone said to someone else, "What do you think
people on vacation want?"

And the other person said, "I don't know.
Nuts, maybe? Let's say nuts." And one of
those people was named Perry.

At some point Perry's course-corrected and realized it had to offer other, non-nut merchandise to the weary traveler, and so it has since expanded to include all kinds of Maine-ish souvenirs and gewgaws and lobster onesies as well as a wide variety of fudge. Do you remember the real talk we had a few paragraphs ago about lakes? Similarly, can we now all agree, as adults, that fudge is repulsive? Look, I appreciate I am not an expert. As I have written before, I do not have a sweet tooth (I have an alcohol molar). But I have seen the same astonishing cake- and candy-themed competition shows that you have. Chefs are making impossible, beautiful things out of sugar: candy floss clouds and fantasy cities of marzipan and cakes that look like Boba Fett helmets and massive double cheeseburgers and a giant shrimp cocktail. OK: those last ones are weird and gross. But they prove that you can make sugar look like anything; no one is forcing you to make it look like **fudge**. I don't need to tell you what fudge looks like. But I will anyway: it looks like a dark, impacted colon blockage that a surgeon has to remove to save your life. Stop eating it.

Like a lot of roadside stands from the early twentieth century, Perry's doubled as a kind of museum of curiosities. I guess the idea was that any travel, no matter how close to home, should put you in contact with the worldly and exotic. Since there was not much of that in Maine, Perry's, like many of its ilk, adorned itself with taxidermy, both natural and rogue. Some of it has been retired. The twin bear cubs posed as boxers with gloves sewn onto their paws, for example, disappeared when Perry's briefly closed in 1997. That's also when the large model elephant (Hawthorne II) that once stood outside Perry's got sold and put atop the movie theater in Belfast. But there is still an imposing stuffed albatross and a full alligator skin hanging on the wall and a small mummy in the glass case beneath the cash register, staring up at the Mexican jumping beans and chunks of fool's gold available for impulse purchase.

The centerpiece of the collection is a taxidermied gorilla someone dubbed "Ape-Braham" in order to correct any accidental delusion that this was an actual, serious endeavor at natural history. Ape-Braham was recently restored from his former moldering condition, and he looks great as he stands there at the front of the store, his eyes looking forlornly upward, inches from the new drop popcorn ceiling as if to say, "Welcome to Maine, children! Begin thinking about death!"

Upon every visit to Perry's, I make sure to browse the Maine Humor section. "Maine Humor" is a very specific subset of comedy. It consists mostly of men with flinty, Down East accents giving bad directions to people from away. Also acceptable are stories about being chased by bears, defecated upon by seabirds, and near drownings. Punishment by nature is a common theme, appropriate to the state, and unflappability in the face of the same is another. Perry's Maine Humor section has many books and CDs with titles like **A Moose and a Lobster Walk into a Bar . . .** and **Suddenly the Cider Didn't Taste So Good** and **Bangor? I Hardly Know Her!** I had to make that last one up, because I guess the Maine humorists are just not doing their jobs.

Maine humorist John McDonald opens his CD, **Ain't He Some Funny!**, with a warning that if you are expecting to laugh at what you are about to hear, you are missing the point of Maine Humor. He posits that you should look forward instead to a kind of low inner chuckling, so dry and so deep inside you that you may not realize it is happening. Thus my problem with Maine Humor. Comedy that abdicates its requirement to be funny is objectionable to me on two levels: first, it's lazy; and second, that's **my** thing.

The archetypal examples of Maine Humor are the "Bert and I" stories, recounting the non-adventures of a lobsterman ("I") and his sternman, Bert. A typical "Bert and I" story (and the first) involves Bert and I starting their boat, the **Bluebird**. Then they go out to sea. Then they get stuck in fog. Then they get hit by a larger boat. The end. All of this is punctuated by dry asides and incomprehensible local terminology and vocal imitations of lobster boat engines made from breath and spittle that my wife finds disgusting and scary. There are many books and albums of these stories, and I have eventually come to enjoy them. Sometimes they actually **are** funny in a way that is very quiet and very occasional. But they are always hypnotic, the storyteller's twisty, alien accent devolving into white noise. There is one live recording of "Bert and I" in which I can truly make out only every tenth word or so. Same with the audience, I'm pretty sure. But you hear the cadence of story in the stream of nonsense mouth sounds, and the dead pauses that intimate where jokes **should** be, and then you hear the audience, out of confused obligation, fill in the silence with laughter.

It's a kind of genius, akin to the anticomedy of Andy Kaufman, and doubly so because it's all bogus. There is no Bert and there is no I. That live recording was by Marshall Dodge, who was from New York. He and his college classmate Robert Bryan (also from New York) started collecting Maine stories when they were at Yale in the '50s, then recorded them in their own imitations of Maine accents to great acclaim through the '70s: an act of cultural appropriation and weird white minstrelsy that would not be rivaled in sheer gall until the advent of Larry the Cable Guy. I've watched what few videos of Dodge exist on YouTube. He's a powerfully skilled storyteller, and whoever he was in truth hid behind his dark eyes and hollow-cheeked deadpan.

Dodge claimed that he had spent no more than a week in Maine before the first "Bert and I" recording. I know this from his obituary: he was struck by a car while riding a bicycle in Hawaii, an inversion on every level of the first **Bluebird** story, in that Hawaii is warm, a bicycle goes on land, and when the **Bluebird** sank, Bert and I survived. Marshall Dodge didn't. He was forty-five years old.

I was forty-five myself when I learned this fact. But I was haunted by Maine Humor long before that. Summer after summer through my twenties and thirties as we stopped at Perry's I would find myself staring at this section with a mix of repulsion and relief. Whatever was happening in my career at that time, first as a writer, then as a performer . . . whatever anxieties I felt about my doubtful qualifications and fortunes, I could always console myself: **At least I am not** this. **At least I am not a middle-aged, Yale-educated phony peddling half-funny stories about the state of Maine.**

Please put this book down for a moment to appreciate my incredible mastery of literary irony. I'll just be over here curling into a ball, trying to disappear forever.

A Kingdom Property

There is one more thing I want to tell you about Perry's Nut House. One recent summer, taped to the door was a sign. It was a plain sheet of printer paper, with the following words handwritten on it in angry Sharpie: "NO BATHROOM." This was a lie. Of course there is a bathroom in Perry's Nut House: it is a **building**. Having a bathroom was probably the whole point of Perry's Nut House when it began in the '20s: lure travelers in with the bathroom, then while you have them, sell them on the fudge. It was a perfect fudge-out/fudge-in economy. If you did not appreciate that particularly brilliant allusion, hand this book to your nine-year-old.

If it were being honest, the sign on the door of Perry's Nut House should have said this:

Yes. There is a bathroom. But you cannot use it. Because we hate you. Because we live here all the time. For ten months of darkness we endure. We stare down the lonely cold. And just when it starts to get warm again, you **show up. You show up with**

demands: for lobster rolls and driving directions, housecleaning and landscaping, life experiences and fudge. And yes, this is a voluntary agreement. We are willingly selling you these things because we need your money to keep our houses warm when you aren't here. And we will admit that we take a certain pleasure in selling to you and then watching you eat a substance that looks like human feces. (Fudge.) But it is still difficult. And over the years, the anger we feel over your making us work during what is, after all, our summer too becomes hard to bear. So we take our small vengeances where we can. Cont'd on back of sign. Please turn over.

(Page 2)

So no. You may not use the bathroom. In fact, we would rather your child vomit on our front steps than let you use the bathroom. Signed, the management of Perry's Nut House.

I know the second page of the sign I just made up is true because I saw it happen. That same summer the sign appeared, my wife and

I watched a young mother comfort her crying four-year-old daughter as she heaped sick
upon Perry's doorstep. And in that moment
I felt I could hear the spirit of that ancient
building, hissing to itself contentedly. "Yes . . .
good!" it seemed to say, voicing Maine resent-
ment logic at its finest: "Vomit all over **ME**!
That will teach **YOU**!"

So yes, Maine is called Vacationland. But
what it should really say on that sign above
the Piscataqua River Bridge is "MAINE:
PUTTING THE SPITE IN HOSPITALITY
SINCE 1820."

There is tremendous wealth in Maine, especially on the coast, and tremendous pov-
erty, and in the summer, when wealth comes
to visit, they are literal neighbors. You can't
see the biggest old money estates. But drive
along one peninsula road and you will see the
tall privet hedges that conceal them; and
then a handful of new money mansions that
want to be seen, their too-perfect, computer-
designed gables slashing the skyline like bad
CGI; and then next to them tiny, crumbling
saltwater farmhouses—just boxes really—

their dooryards ramshackled with junk and weeded-over boat trailers, loitering chickens, the husk of a purple VW pickup truck.

Once my wife and I went to an estate auction at a big, flaking white-shingled house a few towns over from where we were staying. This was the family seat of an old Maine working family whose name you would know if you spent any time there in the summer and needed plumbing or gas or plowing or repair or gravel or any other life-necessity you failed to study in college. Basically every true Mainer on this particular peninsula is either a Carter or a Gray or an Astbury or this one other name that I will not reveal, to protect their privacy. This family had run a general store for decades, but it had closed years ago. And with no heir willing to maintain it, the family home was now for sale, all of its contents seemingly exhaled into the driveway in one big, final death rattle of a breath.

Watching things decay, decline, and end is a popular Maine hobby, so locals and summer people alike had come and posted up their folding camp chairs to watch the auctioneer sell off this pair of old side tables, this box of tools, these cassette tapes, this captain's chest, this generator, this mysterious and dangerous-looking piece of farm equipment, this length of heavy rope.

There were also some obvious fellow New Yorkers there: a clutch of two affluent, super-liberal families, the guys both wearing porkpie hats and the women in huge sunglasses. They were adults of the flashy/dress-too-young kind where you don't know what the story is—it's either two hetero couples or two same-sex couples, with the two nineteen-year-old daughters orbiting them, whispering around in their vintage dresses, the tattoos of math equations on their arms, who are either sisters or lovers.

The Porkpies smiled too brightly as each item was heaved off the pile and brought to the auctioneer by an army of husky young men in shirts without sleeves. An empty book-case; a secretary with spindly legs; a crate of antique Clicquot Club root beer bottles; a box of old toys including a toy ambulance with a doll's hand shoved in the back; old license plates; Limoges. The auctioneer would try to talk up everything, but toward the end of the day his patter deflated. At one point an old ten-speed was brought before him. "We have here a bicycle," he said. "It's just a good, good, good bike."

On the one hand I sympathized with the auctioneer. The sheer volume of stuff was overwhelming. But mostly he was terrible. He either didn't know much about what he was selling, or he didn't care. As he got worn out and bored, and as the Porkpies and the other few bidders began to sense his surrender, beautiful old bureaus and pressed-back dinner chairs were going for tens of dollars. He had the hand-painted general store sign that once announced the family name in town, and he let someone steal it for something like a hundred dollars. The family had entrusted him to get as much money out of the house as he could, and he was basically throwing its bones out into the road for the Porkpies to bring back to New York and mount in their apartment as a twee novelty. It was a miserable thing to observe. Especially as I was presently losing to them in a bidding war on a box of old bow ties and ascots.

I didn't think I was as bad as them. But then,

the most compelling villains always think they are the heroes. That was the secret to the longevity of the computer ads I was in: the PC thought he was there to help the Mac become a better, more boring computer.

By the time of the Porkpies and the auction, we had already stopped staying with my father-in-law and started renting a house in Maine. It was a fancy house in a fairly fancy town on this peninsula, the kind of large old manor that has a name. But I will call it what the owner, a retired surgeon, called it: a Kingdom Property. I took it at the time to be some specific real estate term, but I've never seen or heard that phrase again.

The former surgeon and his wife lived in the Kingdom Property in the winter, but rented it out during the summer. It had black gables and bone-white shingles, with two additions, one from the '40s, the other from the '80s, sprawling out from its one-hundred-year-old enduring core. It presided at the top of a grassy hill. A winding gravel drive led up to it, colonnaded on either side by tall, wispy pines. Its front lawn overlooked the bay. Its back lawn was dozens of acres of protected woodland and fields. Some of the fields were unmowed, and at twilight the tall grass was full of deer and mosquitoes. Other fields were rented out to a man with cows, the grass kept short by the chew and trod of his micro-herd of Belted Galloways.

There was an old red barn in the back with unused milking stations on the first floor and on the second, a strange little three-quarter-sized tennis court, its painted green surface dotted with bat guano. And the kitchen in the main house had an Aga oven: a red and black hunk of English enameled cast iron that is on all the time, whether in use or not, regardless of the temperature. The owners offered to turn it off completely for the hot summer weeks we rented the house, but we refused because the Aga was wasteful and beautiful, and this was our summer of waste and beauty. The house was much bigger than we needed and cost more than could be justified by clear-eyed reason. But I was still sitting on some television commercial money, and I was willing to throw it all at this house because the first time my wife saw it, she cried.

Once a week, as part of the rental, a woman

and her daughter and her daughter's friend came to clean the Kingdom Property. One early evening we came back from a drive from some other part of Maine where we had been doing nothing all day. The woman and her daughter and her daughter's friend weren't quite finished cleaning the kitchen yet. My children and I waited in the dining room, and my children were mad about it. To be honest, so was I. I didn't want to be there with the sounds of actual work surrounding us, reminding me that the Kingdom Property did not clean itself, but that I was paying other human beings to deal with the food waste and dank towels I had littered behind me. But I knew to push this feeling deep, deep down into a shame compartment to revisit later. My children did not. They were little. They did not want to wait for dinner. And no, they did not want to go out **again** to the clam and burger stand to eat one third of **another** twelve-dollar clam roll and then throw the rest away because they were lying about being hungry in the first place, they just wanted ice cream.

"Why can't the cleaning people just leave?"

they said out loud, right there, as we realized that the daughter or the daughter's friend had just walked into the hall behind us. She had heard it all. She was holding my children's clean sheets, which she had washed.

She couldn't have been much older than sixteen. Less than a decade separated her and my oldest, but also, as we stood there, much more. The daughter or daughter's friend's eyes met mine for a flicker, then looked away. I guessed she was busy shoving feelings of her own away, shames and angers that I could not fathom across that sudden, nauseating chasm of class and privilege. **We're not what you think!** I wanted to tell her. **I'm not fancy! I only went on television by accident!** But I knew what I was: the villain in a Stephen King novel. I wanted to die. Specifically, I wanted to be murdered by a sentient antique car being driven by a rabid Saint Bernard, because that is what I deserved.

Even among the summer people there are tensions. When you put enough affluent white people into a closed system, they will turn on each other eventually. That same summer, my wife signed up both of our children for lessons at the nearby yacht club—sailing for our daughter, rowing for our son. She did this because she had taken sailing lessons there herself as a child, and she hated it. She felt out of place and under-rich and scared, and I guess she wanted our children to have similar trauma. It worked: my son got bullied.

I had never been in a yacht club before. The boathouse itself was open to the water: all sun and air in the big open doors and glossy dark wood paneling within. It was handsome, comfortable, and shabby, as were the members of the club, including the young people who ran the summer sailing school. I remember going to California for the first time and being struck not merely by how casually vain and superficial and mellow everyone was, but more how well and comfortably they wore these clichés. They lived a life without a single second guess, and I goggled at it. To live that way, without constant self-interrogation and panicky doubt, filled me with envy.

The preppies of the yacht club were the same way. They wore scuffed boat shoes and popped collars and deep tans that advertised their casual confidence that cancer was for other people. I don't even want to call them "preppies" because it's such a trite and ancient term. But they would probably call **themselves** preppies, and if melanoma can't win an argument with them, what chance would I have? They scared me. Growing up, I would spend winter vacations reading **Alpha Flight** on the floor of John Lin's bedroom. The preppier kids would go away and come back with lift tickets still pinned to their parkas like little merit badges of assholism. You know my story and what I look like: I was no child of the streets. But even so, I didn't know what a lift ticket was until I was in my thirties. I didn't know why these boys had these negative raccoon masks around their eyes where the snow-amplified sun could not reach them through their goggles. And they were fine not telling me, as I did not exist in their world. I was a ghost to them, shimmering in from another dimension in a too-tight Opus the Penguin T-shirt and carrying an Advanced Dungeons and Dragons manual that, I can confess now, I could not really follow. Now in the yacht club I was reminded of how I felt that time some friend of a friend dressed in all Polo somehow got invited over to my house for a group VHS screening of **The Evil Dead**.

"His parents **must** have money," he apparently confided later to our mutual Dead-ite friend. "Why doesn't he get some better clothes?"

One of the moms in my son's rowing class had a long blond ponytail. The day we dropped my son off, she introduced herself to me. She pointed out her son, whose own blond hair had been bleached impossibly even blonder by the sun. She explained he and the other two boys in the rowing class who were not my son had essentially grown up together every summer here in Maine. She also mentioned she had two older blond kids who are twins, a brother and a sister. She told me the town she lived in in Massachusetts— an even more affluent and suburby suburb than Brookline. She told me that her husband managed a hedge fund and could only get to Maine on the weekends. "It's so great that you can be here all the time with your kids," she said. "What do you do?"

She had other questions. She wanted to know: Where were we staying? Did we rent?

Or did we own? How long had we been coming up? How well did we know the town? I knew what was happening: it was a standard status/wealth scan, to determine if I was sufficiently human. I knew I would not pass. In the past I could rely on my appearances on public radio to excuse my lack of wealth: being on **This American Life** is like being a monk—you may have to sleep on straw and wear the same tattered robe made of tote bags every day, but you are acceptable in polite society because you are sacrificing for a greater cause.

But now, as she asked her questions, I realized something surprising. I had answers. Answers that might actually be meaningful to her. In fact, I was a recognizably famous minor television personality. True, I probably didn't have the kind of money a hedge fund husband would find impressive, but I did have enough for once not to give a feces about her opinion of me. I simply said that I was an unspecified self-employed person who happened to be renting the fanciest house in fancy town, and then I stopped saying anything. I delighted in the darting panic behind her smiling eyes as she tried to solve the puzzle. Let someone else tolerate ambiguity for once.

For this reason, the yacht club was a wonderful experience until the bullying started, which was the end of that first day. Was it bullying? It's hard to say. Eight-year-olds are unreliable narrators, and it was not surprising that my son would feel excluded among a group of boys who had been summering together since birth. Maybe it was just some light picking-on. But the result was the same: tears at the end of the day, and at the end of the next day too, and the next, and me gripped with powerless rage.

Whereas with Ponytail Mom I had **all** the answers, now I had none of them. My experience with bullying was so minimal. As earlier recounted, I was mostly left alone when I was a prime bully target. My one flirtation with **being** a bully was when I would make fun of Elliott Kalan, a sweet movie and comic book obsessive at **The Daily Show**. I would routinely knock over the piles of comic books on his desk. Or I would walk by and pick up a souvenir Iron Man mask from his desk and declare that it was mine now, and then casually drop it in the hallway as soon as I left his office. It was a lot of fun, my geek-on-geek bullying. It was so much fun that it escalated. One time I threw my sneakers at him in the hallway, barking at him, "Get lost, nerd!" It felt great. But as my Saucony hit the apex of its arc, I saw Elliott's eyes, and I understood something: this game **was** a lot of fun, but only **for me**. Because I was on-camera talent and Elliott was not, he had to go along with my hilarious meta-commentary on bullying as performance art whether he liked it or not. That's what made it, you know, **actual bullying**. The second half of that sneaker throw was horrible, even more so because the pleasure of the first half was so electric, addictive, and unpunishable.

That is not something that is easy to explain to an eight-year-old: that there is no fighting back. There are no words or fists that can undo the pain caused by teasing, because their power lies in numbers, initiates allied against a lone outsider. And also fighting is terrible and scary and would make my son look crazy, and I don't know how to even form a fist that would hurt someone other than me on contact. Even though I wanted to punch every face in the world right then.

So the bullying went on, and I asked him to endure it. I spoke to the instructors, but they were barely out of their teens, and their eyes would drift. They were ill-equipped and uninterested and entrenched in the yacht club world; my son was also a ghost to them. It did not get better.

As the second week of rowing began I had to beg my son to keep going and see it through. If your children are not in physical danger, if something is just unpleasant, you can't give them permission to quit. First of all, not everything in life is unpleasant, but most of it is, and certainly **all** of the things that lead to real and lasting pleasure are. Second, if you give your child permission to quit, then later they will give **themselves** permission to quit. And we all know those people.

So I encouraged him to endure. "But today," I said, "I think you should wear this shirt."

I handed him the T-shirt he got at his last birthday party at the indoor rock-climbing gym in Brooklyn. He got the shirt because he was the only one to climb to the top of the wall.

I said to my son, "Before I say what I have to say, I have to ask you: do you mind if I say one swear word in front of you?"

He said he did not mind.

So I said, "You have to remember that those three boys all know each other very well. But they don't know you at all. They know nothing about your world or what you can do. Their lives are small. You can tell by how they act. But you live in the largest city in North America. So I think you should wear this shirt. And if they pick on you today, just tell them your name. Tell them you live in Brooklyn, New York, and you got this shirt for climbing a wall when no one else could, so you don't need to take any shit from them."

As I laid out my advice for him, as my own confidence crested, so did his. A smile began on his face and had **just** reached his eyes for the first time in days. And then I said the word "shit." And it all turned to shit. **Yes**, my son had technically given me permission to say a swear word, but only because all little kids want to say yes to their dads. In fact, I bullied him into it. The accurate answer would have been, **Please don't say "shit" in front of me, Dad, because dads are not supposed to say "shit" to their eight-year-old sons. Not unless they are slamming their hand in a door. And when you say "shit," it means there are no rules anymore. Anything can happen. I used to think they were just mean, but now maybe those kids will murder me today.**

After I swore, my son's face grew ashen with terror and then resignation. "I don't want to wear that shirt," he said. And he went and sat silently in the car, accepting his fate. I had forever deranged his internal life with a thoughtless few words. The legacy of Dump Jail continues.

On the last day of rowing lessons at the yacht club, I went to pick up my son. He was not particularly happy it was the last day. He had stopped crying days ago, and he now climbed into the car with the dead, thousand-yard stare that kids get when they decide that this is just how life is going to be forever. That they are just going to survive.

Before we drove away, Ponytail Mom walked up. Smiling. She had figured out my

Daily Show connection by then, and while Hedge Fund Husband probably had a few things to say about how mean the show was to the poor billionaires who had ruined the world economy a few years before, she was reliably blue-statey enough to want to be friends.

She said, "I just wanted to say good-bye!"

"Good-bye," I said.

And that would have been it. I promise you now, as I told my wife later, that I would have said nothing more. But she **asked**. "Did your son have a good time?"

"Well," I said, "since you asked."

I told her my son did not have a good time. I acknowledged that eight-year-olds are unreliable narrators, so who knows what really happened. But apparently her son and the other boys in the rowing class ganged up on him a few times and excluded him a few other times, and it made him feel terrible. And the instructors didn't help, and we all ended up feeling really powerless and bad. So even if I was wrong about the details of what happened, I thought we were all glad it was over.

She said, "Oh no. There must be some

mistake. My son would never do something like **that**."

I said, "I understand, and maybe he didn't. But on another note, I feel I should tell you that I saw your older kids, the twins, in the parking lot yesterday. They were having a full-on fist-fight. I watched your twin son kick his twin sister directly in the center of her chest, causing her to fall flat on her back in the dirt of the driveway. Then he stood on top of her. That's when I suggested that they break it up."

She said, "Oh **no**! The twins are so **physical** with each other. I'm always telling them to go easy, go easy! But my husband says it's just normal!"

I said, "Well, your husband is not around very much. It would be easy for him to miss this. He also works in hedge funds, the most self-congratulatory, macho sector of investing that nonetheless underperforms the S&P 500 and which nearly destroyed the world by driving demand for bad mortgage derivatives in pursuit of more wealth for the super rich. (I read a magazine.) The point is: villains never think of themselves as villains, and white dudes always think of themselves as heroes.

I myself once threw my sneakers at Elliott Kalan and thought it was brilliant meta-humor. But then I saw the hurt and helplessness in Elliott's eyes as my sneakers thunked against his shoulder, and I realized that physically and emotionally attacking people is **not** normal. At all. Ever. Good-bye."

I did not say that last part about her husband. But I did say the rest.

We no longer rent the Kingdom Property. The retired surgeon and his wife put it up for sale a couple of summers later, and there was no way we could afford it. The time in our lives and bank accounts for beautiful waste at the top of the hills and town society had come to a close. It had been inevitable. The television commercials were over. Even if they had continued I would never have made the kind of generation-spanning wealth that accrued to hedge fund husbands and ponytail moms. Sometimes, not knowing what my next job will be, I lie awake at night. I always find it comforting to know that maybe, in that suburb of Boston, that woman also lies awake, because a person from television knows that her children are mean. Then I fall into petty slumber.

The IT Guy for
<u>Duck Dynasty</u>

But recently we did buy a house in Maine. It is a less fancy house in a less fancy town, a boatbuilding community farther out on the peninsula's jagged coast. My wife emailed me a listing she found for a three-bedroom house on a flat, muddy bay. It looked pretty good. We went out and saw it. It looked pretty good in person too. So we bought it, with about as much deliberation as you put into the snap decision to buy a lump of fool's gold at the Perry's Nut House cash register.

Buying a home is always an impulse buy. It's an impossible thing for your brain to absorb fully: to warp your whole emotional and financial life around the shape of this absurd physical thing, this new collection of problems and regrets, ants and undiscovered mold, bad drainage, and cracked foundations that will be your burden until you sell it or it kills you. A thirty-year mortgage is hilarious when you are young and you don't even remember what day it is; it's a grim thing when you are older and see that this debt is a bright, un-ignorable line from the now of your life to its addled decline.

There is that moment at the closing meeting with the various attorneys where you realize: **I don't need to do this. I don't need anything. I can run out of this office and go live in an old hollow tree stump.** But you do not walk away because if you've gotten this far there is only forward. You've given up your apartment and gotten the loan and now you are going to trade this check with "ALL YOUR MONEY" written on it for some vague sense of progress in your life. Or else you know that your wife wants to die in a house in Maine, and you are definitely going along for **that** ride, and if it does not start now it will start next year, and this place looks pretty good, so sure, throw that house in the Perry's Nut House bag and let's get out of here. I don't need a receipt.

This is the reason that we have been letting the garbage rot in rural western Massachusetts. Because we don't go there. We go to our house in Maine. Thus we come to the central conflict of my life and this book, which is this: **I OWN TWO SUMMER HOMES.**

Are you enjoying my very relatable book of essays and reflections?

When I first started telling these stories onstage, my friend John Roderick back-announced my performance by saying to the audience, "Ladies and gentlemen, the white privilege comedy of John Hodgman." It was a painful but fair assessment. Our summer home dilemma is not a problem by any reasonable human definition of that word. But it is still an untenable, unaffordable situation, and the solution is obvious and inevitable: sell the house in Massachusetts. But so far I have not done it, because it is hard. It is hard to say good-bye to a landscape I love, to this last connection to my mom, to a place where we raised young children and were young ourselves. It is hard to clean out a house, to go down into the basement where all the old toys are boxed away. I imagine just opening a box of toys will cause me to double over in tears. I cannot imagine taking them to the dump and adding them to that sad altar along the low wall by the garbage hole. If I did it, I think I would then just walk into the hole and fall forever. And so all that hoard of our kids' past and our past and my mom's past remains hidden there, in an empty house, which I am hoarding as well, waiting for a time when I am braver.

Also Maine means admitting something. It is easy to have dinner with Black Francis in rural western Massachusetts and think you're cooler than you've ever been in your life. Maine does not support this delusion. There are very few cool indie bands roving the Down East coast of Maine, and Maine's population is the oldest in the Union. On our peninsula the young people tend to flee for Portland or points away, leaving their parents alone and embittered. Or if they stay, it may be to work at fishing or lobstering on Deer Isle. I have seen the young sternmen and -women when they come ashore for beer and premade subs at the market in Stonington. They have a competent swagger, but their eyes gaze with a dead calm. They are confronted with harsh demands both physical and existential. I don't think you could spend one season heaving crate after crate of writhing sea insects off the cold floor of the ocean and still be called young, even if you just turned nineteen.

And then there are the retirees, who are plentiful in our town. They live here full-time or part-time, or visit to learn how to build wooden boats. Some are prosperous, but not at all like the preppies of the yacht club. Mostly they are friendly and thrifty and live in small houses for which they saved carefully. They have hobbies and routine walks and road association meetings until they pass away or move to the assisted living facility two towns over, where they smartly put down a deposit years ago.

Our house was built by a retired carpenter, whose career had robbed him of a couple of fingers, and his wife, a quilter and crafter. They had a business making and selling "primitives"—new pieces of furniture that are designed to look like antiques. The house was the same: built ten years ago to look two hundred years old by the carpenter himself, with iron door latches and a huge cooking fireplace in the wooden-beamed "keeping room." They had planned to spend the rest of their lives there, but they changed their mind.

The house stands above a shallow muddy bay. When we first saw it, the bay was barely visible through the screen of trees and mosquitoes. It was low tide and slimy with rockweed and so it made me think of my bog back in rural western Massachusetts. The house sits at the end of a road that we share with a small colony of other small houses hiding elsewhere in the woods. The road is gravel and dirt and privately maintained. It is topped with a material called rotten rock. I am told that that is the good stuff.

The first week we spent in our new/old house in Maine we had a bad mosquito problem and no furniture. We would hide in the kitchen, leaning on the counters. My wife was in bliss, and I was in despair. She had spent the first decade and a half of our marriage in Massachusetts. As much as she enjoyed it (or lied about enjoying it), it was always my mom's world and then mine. It was right and fair now to move to her world. But when I woke up in this unknown country on a mattress on the floor, I felt like a mail-order groom.

One afternoon a man appeared at our door. He was an older, hobbitish man in seersucker shorts. He said his name was Percy, and he was there to invite us to a party. His eyes were bright and clever, and the whole thing had a fantasy novel quality to it. So when he suggested we join him at his house next door for a cocktail with the rest of the road association, I said yes. I felt I had a pretty good chance of eating some magical cakes or being transformed into a donkey.

The next day my wife and children and I dressed up (that is, wore socks) and walked on the soft bed of pine needles through the trees to Percy's little cottage. It was only a few steps from ours, but I had never noticed it before. Part of me wondered if it had even been there yesterday. And then we walked inside, and the fantasy novel turned into a horror novel.

I have since come to know and adore my neighbors. They have only been kind and they are all interesting and accomplished people. They have never burned our house down during the off-season and I hope they won't after they have read this account of my first experience of them, colored as it was by my own insecurities at the time, and also maybe Percy had enthralled me with the dark magic of the undead.

So with that preface I will say: walking through Percy's door was like waking an ancient pack of vampires. All of our neighbors are older than we are, and all turned at once as my little family entered the darkened kitchen. The sunlight from the door behind us lit up their faces and glowed in their eyes. Some of the older pairs of eyes fixed upon our children with surprise and dawning memory. It was as if we had presented them with a pair of dolls from their own childhoods that they had thought long lost. **I remember you**, their faces seemed to say. **I thought we had burned you when the scarlet fever came.**

My son and daughter looked up and begged with their eyes to be allowed to run away as fast as possible. I granted that permission, and once they both fled, I turned to accept the martini that Percy offered me and allowed them to pull me into their world.

We all sat on Percy's screen porch. It was high tide on the bay, the water flat and nickel colored. My neighbors introduced themselves. Here was Clark, head of the road association and a retired pastor. Here was his wife, Diane, a retired travel agent. Percy had largely retired from his catering business in Boston but still taught the occasional cooking class in his home for the local ladies of Maine. Dan and Louise were younger. He works at an auction house. She has corgis. As I listened to this I smiled, but locked my eyes onto my wife's. **What have you done to me?** I screamed telepathically. **I don't belong here! I am young! I am cool! This time last year I was getting high in a river making cairns!**

My wife did not hear me. Because there is no such thing as telepathy **or** vampires. And of course, I **did** belong there.

There are times when all the lies you have told about yourself **to** yourself just fall away. In your twenties, you tell yourself the lie that you are unusual, unprecedented, and interesting. You do this largely by purchasing things or stealing things. You adorn yourself with songs and clothes and borrowed ideas and poses. In your thirties, you tell yourself the lie that you are still in your twenties. Many in their forties tell themselves the same lie, until a moment like this, and suddenly you see yourself clearly. Yes, I went to see Public Enemy in a small club in 1990 by myself, which was pretty cool of me; but less cool now that I remember I saw them at Toad's Place in New Haven while attending Yale University. Yes, I shoplifted some off-brand beers and snuck into the London Zoo when I was in my twenties; but only now do I realize that I did so with full, if unconscious, confidence that I would not be executed in the street for doing these things. Yes, my parents came from modest working middle-class families, but I have never truly wanted for anything in my life. I do not say these things to flay myself for my many privileges, just to draw out the truth and see it. I opened this book by apologizing for my beard, but the fact is that we can only grow the beards we can. This is my life, and even my beard is a lie if you look at it plainly. I do **not** look like the Church of Satan's bookkeeper. I look much more like the IT guy for **Duck Dynasty**. And there, on Percy's screen porch, I knew exactly what I was: a forty-five-year-old wealthy white Bostonian who had gone north for vacation, here to a cold dark place, gripping a martini, surrounded by his people but not speaking to them, simply staring over nickel gray cold water that I would never, ever swim in.

When we got home from Percy's house, our

children kept their distance from us. It stayed that way for the rest of the summer. One could argue, as my wife did, that it was just a case of age-appropriate self-individuation. I think they smelled death on us. Either way, our son spent much of his time playing alone in the yard. Our daughter would set out alone on her bike many mornings and ride the two miles into the little town. There is a cemetery there where a famous writer is buried. She would visit his grave and put a little stone on the headstone, as is the custom. Or maybe she danced on it. I don't know. I didn't go with her. She didn't need her old man to go have graveyard fun anymore.

So Thin Is the Skin of My People

The famous writer who is buried in our town also lived there. I had no idea of this when we bought our house. Because he is one of my wife's favorite writers, you might presume that our move to this town was a simple case of spousal manipulation. But she also didn't know. That was the way the famous writer wanted it. He was private. When asked once by the **New York Times** where he lived, he said he lived in a town on the East Coast "somewhere between Nova Scotia and Cuba." I won't tell you either.

My wife was raised by her father to respect the privacy of the people of Maine. Know where the property lines are. Don't ask people about their health. Don't go near lobster buoys because if your boat fouls their lines you will be marked for death. When hiring someone to do a job, don't ask how much it will cost. That kind of curiosity will mark you as an outsider.

And it was true that first summer, when we had to hire people to fill up propane tanks (again!) and do all the other things we couldn't, the very idea of openly trading money for services was treated like a confusing breach of etiquette.

We wanted some trees cut down, for example, so we could see the muddy bay a little and deny the mosquitos some small percentage of still air and damp nesting pools. We followed the rules, naturally. We had a local forest warden come out first. Mostly you can defile your property however you want in Maine. If your neighbor, for example, clear-cuts the forest on his land and erects a goofy giant Lincoln Log house with a golden cupola on it, there is no homeowners' association to step in and police their awful taste. Even if they put a pen out and fill it with llamas and donkeys, that is their strange, private universe they are building, and it must not be disturbed. You must train yourself to not hear or see or smell it. But within seventy-five feet of the shore, state regulations kick in regarding drainage and runoff. You cannot denude the shoreline the way the first generation of ravaging wealthy Bostonians did, casting their perfect lawns to the sea. The forest warden tramped through our small strip of woods, inspecting the trees and their age, measuring their distance from each other, tying bows on those that must be kept; the rest were dead or dense enough to be doomed.

My wife's uncle suggested we call a person named Jerry to cut down the trees. I was told to call, not text or email. I did so and left a voicemail message. It was very quaint and time-travelly. But Jerry did not call back. Days later, we were considering who else to call when Jerry just drove up in his truck. He was a tall, lanky guy in his thirties. His visit amounted to him looking at the woods, saying, "Yup," and then driving away. We didn't discuss money.

Days passed again. We were confused. Had Jerry forgotten about us? Had he gotten another job? Should I put some pressure on him? Is another voicemail enough? Do I need to go so far as to send him a **fax**?

Then that morning we woke up to a buzzing, then that sharp, hollow baseball-bat-crack of a trunk giving way, followed by the cascading tumult and crash of treefall, sounding almost like surf. Jerry had come to cut down our woods. We ran downstairs. It was like Christmas, except in this case Santa has a chainsaw and you get to kill a whole lot of pine trees instead of just one.

Jerry came cutting for two days. Then he disappeared again for a while. Then he came back for a third day. When Jerry was cutting we canceled our morning plans to watch from the screen porch. It was like a monster was crashing through the woods. You couldn't see the monster, only the trees shuddering first at the top, and then collapsing in its wake. Every now and then, though, we could hear Jerry laugh. Or a falling tree would reveal him with his boots and his gloves and his chainsaw. Maybe I saw him wearing eye protection, but I can't be sure. He was just alone, unaided, happily fighting with a forest.

Eventually Jerry cut up all the trunks and stacked the wood for us and went away. Some days later, almost as an afterthought, he came back with a number on a piece of paper. I don't remember it, but it was very low. In honor of ancient technology I wrote him a check, which he put in his jeans pocket and left. We barely spoke.

At first I thought Jerry was so distant because we were from away. But after watching him cut I decided that it was simply that he didn't have time to waste on us. He liked cutting down trees (and whatever else he liked when he went back to his own private world) and he was not going to spend a lot of time opening up to me when the days in Maine shorten so quickly.

Eventually my wife and I began to suspect that her father's reverence for privacy, his fear of being branded an outsider, was really a trick he used to mask his own desire to be left alone. Which is, of course, what makes him native.

The famous writer was not a native Mainer. He was from New York. But he found in Maine the same thing my father-in-law and my wife discovered and that Jerry was born into: a love of the natural world, and a desire to keep human interaction to a minimum. He was already famous when he worked in New York, but he did not want to be. When people would come to see him in New York, he would flee his office using the fire escape. When he moved to Maine he avoided most weddings and other large gatherings. He raised chickens. Once he wrote about how his hens had lain surplus eggs, but he would not take them to sell at the town store out of some opaque combination of reticence, shame, and shyness that my wife cannot quite figure out because he didn't bother to describe it, really. It was as if to describe that part of himself would be the same as pointing out that he was born with a nose and still had it and used it to breathe: needless words.

Look. I'm not going to be cute. You can figure out who I am talking about very easily. You can figure out the name of his town, and then you can find that town, and you can come and murder me and my family.

But you will gain no happiness from doing that, and I trust that you won't. One thing I've learned in the public eye is that if you give people a measure of trust not to invade your privacy, they largely don't. (It helps if you are only book famous and not actually famous. And no matter how close I might have come to being the latter, the fact that I am writing to you now proves I will always actually be the former.)

The famous writer eventually died, and his house was put up for sale without ceremony. He did not want it to become a museum. A married couple who are not famous writers bought it and live there still. And whether out of special respect for their privacy or the famous writer's legacy of same, or just out of decency, the location of this particular local point of interest is not celebrated and definitely not advertised. It's usually not discussed at all. It was a long time before we knew about the house, and longer before we knew where it was. But eventually the information was slipped to us, and we received it as a gift of trust. When my wife's mother came to visit that first summer, she asked that we take her to the famous writer's house to take a picture. My wife told her, "No." This gave my wife tremendous pleasure for many complicated reasons.

When we learned the location of the famous writer's house, we realized we had been driving by it all the time for weeks. Now that we knew, we would not even slow down as we drove by. We would catch little flashes of it in the corners of our eyes, assembling an image of it, piece by piece, into something we could look at in our minds later.

Over time, my wife received more information about the house. She did not ask anyone—she is her father's daughter. She **gleaned**. From many conversations around town, she pieced together a story that grew in the telling each time we drove by. The couple who lived there were older than us. They were childless. The house was getting to be too much for them. They would be selling it soon. But they were waiting for the **right person**. They were waiting for someone who knew how special the house was. The kind of person who reads aloud from the writer's books to her husband in the car, and they both fight off tears, because of the kinship that she feels for this writer and his love of Maine. And when the current owners find that person, they will sell it to her. And it won't matter that she and her husband had just bought a home in the same town and cannot afford a third summer home. Because they were going to sell it to her for a single dollar.

My wife's information was not accurate. First of all, no one told my wife that the house would be sold for a dollar except her own hoping brain. And second of all, the couple who own the house definitely have children, as I would soon learn. My wife's delusion was born only out of an affection for the famous writer, which also extends to his heirs, who still live in town and deserve their privacy. And her affection also extends to the couple who own the house now, whom we've never met, whose own affection for its legacy is shown by their immaculate upkeep of it. It's not a museum, but it is perfectly preserved. Or maybe, unlike us, they are simply not garbage people who **do** deserve to own a home. Whatever the case, I ask only that my neighbors in town do not blame my wife for what I am about to reveal, or for the fact that I've already said too much.

I wasn't going to write about the famous writer at all. But I was thinking of him last summer while sitting on the screen porch. It was the same porch where we had watched Jerry tear through our woods, but now we were in the middle of a different reaping. Two black men, Alton Sterling and Philando Castile, had just been killed by the police in rapid succession in Louisiana and Minnesota, respectively. Their deaths were the most recent iteration of a pattern of similar killings of unarmed people of color stretching shamefully far back, and reaching far nearer in time than most white people wanted to admit. If you were not a victim of the pattern—and statistically speaking, if you are white, you weren't—it was easy not to see it. It was easy to picture the news of each killing as unconnected points, distant and discrete stars out there in space that we could only see fuzzily from a distance, and behind which, we would console ourselves, lurked no angels.

But with the iPhone, Steve Jobs stole the internet from the desktops of the relatively few white nerds who had previously dominated its user base and put it in the hands of millions more. And many of those hands—soon the majority in the US—are brown. There is no privacy anymore. With a civilian surveillance device in everyone's hands, the pattern could not be hidden, not even in Maine. We had video. We could see the similarity of the killings as they tumbled one after one into our feeds, the specific details, mitigating circumstances, and tragic split-second decisions blurring into what couldn't be denied: a pattern, self-similar and replicating, seemingly infinite and seemingly unstoppable . . . an ugly fractal of injustice with cruel edges, twisting in on itself, choking out life.

You **had** to see it, though many tried not to and tried hard. In different parts of the world, protests sprung up to defend the humanity of the specific people who had been killed, as well as non-white people everywhere. Some white people found that standing up for the humanity of non-white people somehow threatened **their** humanity, and made a point of saying so on the internet. They fought the Black Lives Matter idea with a fervor that was unseemly and dumb. It reminded me of the offense I took when I realized I would not live forever: how dare you suggest I am not the hero of this story? I am a straight white man! I have been right at the center of this culture for a long time, and now you ask me to be quiet for **a few days** to listen to someone **else's** experience? Look, I know that you will soon outnumber me, and my ability to define reality will soon disappear, but not yet!

I am still here! YOU NEED TO LISTEN TO ME THAT **MY** LIFE MATTERS BECAUSE I AM SECRETLY NOT SURE OF IT ANYMORE! I'M STILL COOL! I'M STILL RELEVANT! HERE ARE HORRIBLE, BADLY DESIGNED MEMES TO PROVE IT! It wasn't just aging guys like me anymore; it was as if **all** of Whiteness was going through a desperate midlife crisis.

I was ashamed. Even after a summer in Maine, at the tannest I would ever get, you could see the blue veins in my forearms, so thin is the skin of my people. But I felt worse because I knew where I was. The killings and their aftermaths were on the internet. The internet was in my lap on my screen porch in Maine, 94 percent white as of 2013. And if I closed my laptop, I could make it all vanish.

Maine is a tolerant place. It has a wide range of political thought and lifestyles within it, generally moderated by a "let's not talk about politics (or pretty much anything)" policy suitable to the region's temperament. The coast has a leftward lean (where it is not inhabited by Bushes), with our peninsula long attracting artists and freethinkers, including a bakery staffed by elfin, starry-eyed young people that I am pretty sure is a free love cult. Sometime after I first met our neighbors, the non-vampires, I learned that our private, rotten rock road, which I had taken as a symbol of my journey into dull, conservative adulthood, was actually named for Mildred Harris, who with her life partner Fredda Goetz built their house on the road in the 1970s. Fredda was an artist and a Red Sox Fan, Mildred a physical therapist and expert in Jungian analysis. As far as I can tell, they were well liked and their partnership utterly uncontroversial in town. Their final years were spent on their lobster boat ordering their hired captain around as they went out in search of mackerel. I have been on that boat since. It's an honest and unflashy craft, never used for lobstering, purposed unapologetically to spending time while it lasted with beloved things, and I take it as a reminder to never underestimate the cool of your elders. They might be a kickass pair of lesbian superwomen who lived exactly the fuck the way they wanted to, even in what we now consider to be less enlightened times.

What's more, there are sizable communities

of immigrants from Somalia, Rwanda, and other African countries that are invigorating failing towns like Lewiston and offering even additional vibrancy to Portland, a city that is so young and vibrant and cool that it is known as the Portland, Oregon, of Maine.

But this is also true: Maine's governor at this writing is a foul-mouthed bigot who openly accuses black men of crossing the southern border into Maine specifically to sell drugs and have sex with white women. And well before there was the Trump Administration there was the Paul LePage constituency, which also took root in a white, conservative working class who had lost their manufacturing jobs and were watching their kids succumb to an epidemic of heroin. I'm not suggesting that LePage voters are necessarily racist. I would posit that even those of my neighbors who **are** racist would not act upon those prejudices. They would probably offer a person of color from away the same taciturn blank stare they offer me. The difference is that I never have to worry about whether someone is a racist, because I am white. And the racists rarely need to worry about racism either, because, just speaking statistically, there are hardly any other races to see.

I have picked up hitchhikers twice in my life, both in Maine. The first time was a young couple who flagged us down as we were driving the loop road in Acadia National Park. They had gotten lost hiking and were looking for a ride back to the parking lot.

When they got in the car they said, "Are you John Hodgman?"

"Yes," I said.

"Oh, wow," they said, "we are huge fans of your podcast."

I said, "This must be very surprising for you."

"It is!" they said.

"What makes it even stranger," I said, "is that usually it's the **hitchhikers** who end up murdering the **driver**. And not the other way around, like this time!"

It was just another example of the wit and wisdom of me at my finest. I didn't murder them. We met up again later in Brooklyn, because of course that is where they live.

The second time I picked up a hitchhiker was last summer. We were driving out to see my father-in-law. It was a hot day. We were not far from the Kingdom Property and the yacht club when we saw a black woman in her twenties had her thumb out. This was such a profoundly uncommon thing to see that it unnerved us. We worried she was in trouble. She wasn't. She sighed happily as she climbed into the AC of our car.

"Phew," she said. She told us she was going just a few miles up the way to her parents' house.

"Do you not have a car?" I asked.

"Not anymore," she said. "But I usually get a ride. I'm pretty well known around here."

Once in Bar Harbor I saw an older, affluent black couple sitting on the porch of the ice-cream parlor. They were on the same side of the table, facing out toward the town green. They were just silently watching the parade of well-heeled Caucasians walk by. They were sharing a vanilla ice-cream cone. I could not guess what they were thinking about.

Maine is a beautiful place that I paradoxically want to hoard to myself and share with everyone I meet. But that day on the screen porch I thought, shamefully for the first time, about what it would be like to be a non-white person visiting Maine. How it might be glorious and wonderful, but necessarily complicated to see so little of yourself. I knew, shamefully for the first time, that when I closed the internet today, I could go out into my community and never have to think about race for another second of the day. I don't know what about that particular day on the screen porch made me feel this so keenly. I should have known it all along.

That summer I thought about the famous writer in a new way. It won't surprise you to know that he is white, and he wrote about the rhythms of his life in this white place. There is nothing wrong in this: all places and experiences deserve writing about. But what made the writer a greater hero to me in that moment was, unlike so many white men, he wasn't braggy. He never suggested that his experience was heroic, or correct, or even unusual. In fact, it was profoundly usual, beautifully mundane, and merely his to offer. His offering was his insight into the small joys of his particular life, which by extension could help us recognize the small joys that exist everywhere, even outside of Maine. And he offered it humbly. You really should use your detective skills and find his work. He's great.

We who are white men can't change who we are. But we could do worse than to follow what I took that summer as his example: to be aware of and curious about the world around you, to give what you have with neither apology nor self-congratulation. When praise comes to see you, get out on the fire escape. When it's someone else's time to talk, listen. Don't turn your house into a museum. When your work is done, get out of the way.

I resolved to be disciplined in following this lesson. But then someone posted a photo on the internet that made me mad. It was some weeks later, and because it was summer in Maine, my wife had built a huge fire in the fireplace. I was lying on the sofa and I wanted to see what photos people had taken of this part of Maine so I did a search for our peninsula on a popular social media platform. Mostly I found a bunch of rocky beaches and kayaks and docks and buoys and junk. Someone was taking pictures of food and dogs, of course. Someone was posting pictures of their cracked foundation. And then I saw the young couple standing in front of a porch, arm in arm, smiling for the camera. I knew that porch, even if I **had** only seen it in dozens of split-second drive-bys. And in case I wasn't sure, the photo was named, tagged, and pinned on a map: it was the house of the famous writer.

How do I describe this couple without invading their privacy? They were young, white, beautiful, and happy. The account belonged to the beautiful young woman. The caption suggested the handsome young man on her arm was related to the current owners, who clearly did have children after all. I scrolled deeper into her feed. They were clearly about to graduate from college, or had done so recently. They were travelers: here they were in Europe, here they were at an American country club, here they were on a beach, here they were in the mountains, each jaunt posted just days after the last. Either the photos had been stored up, or they were speeding through the world on an insane grand tour.

They were doing nothing wrong. They were reveling in the joys of **their** particular lives, and they were sharing their selfie-triumphs with a verve entirely common to their age. It was wrong for me to think that they were embodying the worst of whiteness: the casual, unquestioning acceptance of good fortune, in the form of money, perhaps, or opportunity, or skin that lets you pass through the world with a smile, or a house in Maine, famous for someone else's work, and passing it off as if you earned it all yourself, or were beyond earning, simply **deserving**. Did they think this way? Who knows? Perhaps they are more woke than I will ever be. Was I any better than they? I was worse, because I was the creep stalking them then and writing about them now. But I could not help but feel desperate and mad. Not only had they revealed the secret of the famous writer's house, but they would possibly live in it one day, and they would not sell it to my wife for a dollar.

I shared this with my wife. She instructed me that I should just forget it, and I should have listened to her. But Handsome Young Man and Beautiful Young Woman haunted me. One evening I went deeper into the feed than I had ever gone before. I was like Ant-Man at the end of **Ant-Man**, shrinking deeper and deeper into the dark microverse, where I finally found a photo, taken at the house, that pushed me over the edge, into a new, previously undiscovered dimension of smallness.

There is a famous photo of the famous writer at work. He is sitting at a manual typewriter in a plain shed, a bare plank for a desk and not even a window so much as a square hole in the wall open to the water and sky. The shed, apparently, is still there. Beautiful Young Woman took a picture of herself sitting at the plank, pretending to write: a replica of the older photo. She placed the two images together. "Here is a photo of the author writing all their famous novels and essays," she wrote. "And here is an old man sitting in the same place."

I saw this, and I did the wrong thing. I scrolled down and left a comment. I will not reveal what I said, because it is a direct reference to the famous writer's work. Oh, it was very clever. My internet comment was literary and oblique, a deft critique of hubris and odious comparison. But all it really was was an insult.

I am the villain of this story. I was a forty-five-year-old man trolling a young woman in her twenties who was simply making a joke. I guess I just wanted to explain to her everything that was wrong with the way she saw the world and was living her life. Just like every other dude on the internet! After all, there is no mansplaining like white mansplaining, because white mansplaining don't stop. My insulting her was an insult also to the famous writer and my own soul. But I won't lie. I did it. I am ashamed to admit that it took me twenty-four hours to delete my comment.

I hope she and her young man have a wonderful time visiting and later owning the house of the famous writer. I am grateful to be reminded of how vigilant I need to be about my skin and its thinness and the responsibilities both entail. I apologize to her for what I said, and I apologize to her and to the owners of the house for apologizing here. I couldn't do it in the comments. Because a few days later, I noticed she had gone private.

You Are Normal People

In the middle of our first summer in Maine, as our children ignored us, something happened. Left to our own devices, my wife and I fulfilled our Caucasian class destiny in the most loathsome way possible. I feel embarrassed even now admitting to you what we did. But I have promised to be truthful, and so I now confess: we bought a boat.

In our defense, I offer that (a) it is not a yacht or anything: just a thirteen-foot rowboat, and (b) we bought it by accident. I'm sure you have also bought a boat by accident, so at the risk of boring you, here is our story.

As July ended, flyers started going up outside the general stores of our town and many more around it. The flyers advertised a charity auction to be held some Saturdays from now to benefit a church whose roof was failing. People had donated many things to be auctioned, but the premier item was a wooden Jimmy Steele peapod.

You don't know what a Jimmy Steele peapod is because you are a normal person. I did not know what it was either. But as conversation spread across the peninsula about the auction and the peapod, I learned. A peapod is a style of rowboat that is about twelve to fifteen feet long and pointed on both ends, like a peapod. (Get it?) It is very typical to this stretch of Maine, because it is very stable and heavy, good in choppy waters and rowable in both directions. It can also take a very rudimentary, boomless sail called a spritsail, which is a word I just learned. Before there were motors, it was the traditional craft of the Maine lobsterman. He would stand up, rowing his peapod into and out of the coves with long oars, hauling up lobster pots, his foot braced flat on the gunwale, which is another word I just learned, without fear of tipping. And then he could bring up the sail and let the prevailing winds carry him back to shore, thus making a living entirely on his own, almost without ever having to see or speak to another human ever in his life, which I am convinced is the secret dream of every person in Maine.

I have mentioned that ours is a town of boatbuilders, many employed by the big former cannery that was transformed in the '60s by the son of the famous writer into a boat-building yard. The son of the famous writer did not want to write. He wanted to design and build wooden boats in the traditional style, and he is famous for doing exactly that. The boatyard along with the boatbuilding school he also helped to found are a double mecca for the weird dads who follow that sort of thing. But the town is also home to many solo wooden boatbuilders, and one of those was Jimmy Steele, whose old workshop still sits at the head of the flat, muddy bay.

Jimmy Steele died in 2007. He built not only boats but also a lot of the homes in town, including Percy's. Everyone has a story about him, and the impending sale of one of his peapods shook them out of people's memories. As you know, I am changing the names of many people in this book, but I **will** identify my neighbor Brian Larkin, because I think he'd enjoy it, and he has taken us out on his own boat to many interesting islands, and if he's wrong about any of this I want him to take the blame. Brian is also a boat-builder. One day he realized he was running low on white oak, which is a kind of wood, I guess. Don't ask me. I am not a builder of traditional wooden boats.

Brian went to Jimmy's workshop and asked his neighbor if he could buy some white oak off of him. Jimmy told Brian he was not in the business of selling fucking lumber, so get out. Brian, who is native to Maine, seemed to anticipate this possible response and, thus, politely got the fuck out.

The next day, Brian was at work when he heard the noise of an engine outside his shop. It was Jimmy Steele in his truck. His truck was full of white oak. Jimmy Steele dumped the wood into Brian's dooryard and said, "**There's** your goddamned wood."

I like to think about what happened in the brain of Jimmy Steele during the hours that passed between Brian getting the fuck out and the dumping of the goddamned wood. I like to think that Brian's simple request made Jimmy angry not merely because it was an intrusion, but because it added a chore to his life that he did not choose for himself. And yet once the request fell upon his brain, he could not stop thinking about it. It became a curse of neighborly obligation that could not be lifted until he dumped the magic wood. And then he would be free again to go back into his solitude and next time not answer the door. I don't know if Jimmy Steele thought that way. But I like to think he did, because that's how I think a lot of the time, and I want to feel normal. And it would prove my maxim about favors, which is the exact opposite of what your encouraging parents have always told you: it does, in fact, **always** hurt to ask.

Brian watched Jimmy dump the wood and said thank you. He asked Jimmy what he owed him, and Jimmy barked at him "**Nothing!**" and drove away.

I obviously wished to see a boat built by such angry and generous hands, so we went to the auction. We were not alone. There must have been fifty or sixty people there, and I am confident they did not come for the rest of the junk that was on offer. It was just old half sets of Candy Land, hair dryers, unmatched ski poles, and other miscellany, all tagged and arrayed on tables in the high school gymnasium. It looked like the last recovered items of a town that had been blown away in a tornado. I swear someone was auctioning a Folger's coffee can full of nickels.

But there was the peapod, just outside the gym in the sun. It was beautiful, every piece of goddamned wood bent and fitted together like the elegant solution to some three-dimensional jigsaw puzzle Jimmy Steele saw in his mind and was compelled to solve. There was speculation over how much it would sell for. One of our neighbors, Heidi, a writer, offered to stake us to a bid of two thousand dollars. She is from Maine originally—Heidi is the one who introduced us to the town, where she and her husband, also a writer, spend the summer. We are very fond of both of them, but even though they also live in New York, and even though we make every promise to see them during the winter, we somehow never do. I suspect this is because Heidi, like my wife, would prefer to pretend the non-Maine portion of her life is not actually happening.

But even Heidi knew her two-thousand-dollar gambit was symbolic only. She figured it would sell for much more than that. And now that I examined its varnished rails and other beautiful boat parts I did not and still do not know, I knew she was right. The minimum bid was listed at thirty-five hundred dollars. Plus, it included a trailer.

My wife felt the same way I did about the peapod. We didn't speak about it. I just knew. It's when we start speaking that the misunderstandings start. I said, "Listen: I can tell that you want this boat. And for some reason, suddenly, so do I. But we both know it is going to get very expensive very quickly once the bidding starts. So here is my suggestion: why don't you make the opening bid? Bid the thirty-five hundred dollars and then stop. We will not win, but then we can watch the bidding play out and enjoy knowing that we had some small part in launching this boat, this beautiful piece of ingenious, practical sculpture, onto whatever waters it travels."

And my wife said, "Once again you have proven that you are America's greatest living storyteller. I will do what you suggest."

She did not say that. She said, "That is stupid. No."

But when the auction finally occurred, we both grabbed folding seats near the front as the auctioneer made short work of all the gymnasium garbage and got to the main event. "We now come to the Jimmy Steele peapod," he said, and everyone in the room took one solid step forward.

Unlike the earlier auctioneer, this one knew his stuff. "Now Jim Steele made 178 peapods over the course of his career. The one we have for auction today is later, number 104, I believe. Before we begin, does anyone know how much the first Jimmy Steele peapod sold for? This would have been in 1964. No? Can anyone guess?"

No one was guessing. I do not know what came over me, but finally I just farted out of my mouth the words, "A hundred dollars!"

The auctioneer turned on me, furious. "Yes," he said/hissed. "That is correct." I had stolen his punch line.

He turned back to the crowd. "The last Jimmy Steele peapod to come up for auction was in 2009. Does anyone know what **that** peapod sold for? Anyone?" A pointed glare at me. "Any guesses from **the expert**?"

I will not lie to you. I knew. And I believe in science. But I am not lying that some telepathic spark that connected me to this angry auctioneer and the boat that was in his charge told me the answer. But I knew not to speak. "I do not know," I lied.

"Ten thousand dollars," he announced, triumphant. The audience murmured in appreciative surprise. But I bet they knew too. This was their world.

Bidding began. I was glad I was not going to buy a ten-thousand-dollar boat today. As advertised the auctioneer opened with a request for thirty-five hundred dollars. It took some time for people to get interested. My wife was still not sold on my poetic first-bid scheme, but through a series of urgent eyebrow movements, I bullied her into raising her paddle. "Thirty-five hundred," she said.

"I have thirty-five hundred. Thirty-five hundred dollars to the woman in the front row. Now who will give me thirty-six hundred dollars? Who will give me thirty-six? Do I hear thirty-six in the back? Thirty-six? Who will give me thirty-six."

No one would give him thirty-six. Finally, the auctioneer shamed a tall man with thick glasses into a bid of thirty-six. "Come on, Dan, surely you will go to thirty-six?"

Dan sighed. He went to thirty-six.

Now, however, my wife was **in it**. Something had flipped in her the moment Dan made the mistake to challenge her. As soon as his limping "six" was out of his mouth, her paddle shot up: "THIRTY-SEVEN!"

Now we had an auction. "I have thirty-seven!" said the auctioneer. "Now who will give me thirty-eight? Dan, will you go to thirty-eight?"

Dan was aggrieved. "I already have a peapod!" he said with a shrug to convey, **What more do you want of me?**

The auctioneer, disgusted with Dan, turned back to the crowd. "Who will give me thirty-eight for this Jimmy Steele peapod? It includes a trailer, a rudder, and the spritsail. It's a piece of history, ladies and gentlemen, so who now will give me thirty-eight? Who will give me thirty-eight? I have thirty-seven here in the front, now who will give me thirty-eight? Thirty-eight, please. Thirty-eight hundred dollars, and Tom, the owner, will drive it to your home. Who will give me thirty-eight?

Who will give me thirty-eight, please? This is a Jimmy Steele peapod. This is the reason we are all here. Who will give me thirty-eight? I'm looking for thirty-eight, please. Who will give me thirty-eight?"

No one would give him thirty-eight. Not one person in the world. Everyone in the gymnasium looked down at their feet and took one solid step backward, leaving only my wife in the glare of a single shaft of white sunlight, angling from the gymnasium window. I did not understand what was happening.

Finally, the auctioneer finished it, like an angry engine that has died at the top of a hill: "Thirty-seven going once, thirty-seven going twice . . ." (Pause for roughly twelve hours.) "SOLD, then"—and he looked at my wife—"to **YOU**."

At that moment, we owned a boat. And at that moment, everyone who had been staring down at their feet looked up and smiled at my wife. A short line grew to congratulate her. "Congratulations," they said, one by one. "A Jimmy Steele peapod for thirty-seven hundred dollars. What a **bargain**. Good for **you**."

She wrote the check out to benefit the

church roof. As Tom hitched up the trailer to his truck to drive the boat home for us, they came up, one by one, smiling and repeating: "Good for **you**. What a **bargain**. A Jimmy Steele peapod for thirty-seven hundred dollars. What a **bargain**. Good for **you**."

This went on for the rest of the summer: people stopping us at the library or the store or the boatyard, commenting on the boat, commenting on the bargain. Some weeks after the auction I was checking our post office box. It's number 117. If you can figure out where we live and Claire at the PO hasn't canceled it by then because we don't check it all winter, you can send me a letter there. But please don't approach me. That would be weird.

I was alone in the little room of metal PO box doors when I got approached. It was the owner of the local inn. I had never met him. We were the only ones there. I swear.

He said, "Are you the one who bought the Jimmy Steele peapod?"

"Yes," I said. "I'm John."

"Right!" he said. "How much did you pay for it again?"

"Um," I said. "I think you know. It was thirty-seven hundred dollars."

"Thirty-seven hundred dollars!" he said. "What a bargain!"

And then he said, "Hey, I want you to meet someone."

I am telling you we were the only ones in the PO box room. But somehow, the innkeeper produced a whole woman. From somewhere behind his back emerged an older, handsome strict-looking woman, and the innkeeper said, "Pam, I want you to meet John. He bought a Jimmy Steele peapod for thirty-seven hundred dollars at auction."

"Well," I said, "my wife bought it actually." I do not feel that white dudes need to take credit for everything, especially when it feels like a couple of locals are playing some weird mind game with me, perhaps as a prelude to murder.

"John," the innkeeper continued. "I want you to meet Pam Steele. Pam is Jim Steele's widow."

Every molecule in the air reversed its charge. I said some polite words to Pam Steele that I don't remember. I was in the living presence of a history that I knew nothing about before I saw this boat, and now I was being judged by that history.

Pam Steele placidly held me with her eyes. "I wanted to meet the person who paid thirty-seven hundred dollars for one of Jim's boats," she said. And then she peered through me for a bit, coming to some silent determination of her own. "Good for you," she said, and then she left the post office.

What is happening? I wanted to say to the innkeeper.

Is this some ritual? Do you do this every year? You hold a bogus auction, and then you trick some couple from away into buying a peapod? And once they make that winning bid do you befriend them? You feed them, fatten them with compliments. You make them feel like they're welcome. And then after some time of Ripening, do you bring them before the Widow for judgment? Do you wait until the end of the summer to Harvest them? Do you sneak into their homes on the eve of the town fair and drug them with strange, pungent

herbs? Do you take them down to the fair-
grounds at dawn where they will awaken,
tied to a stake, surrounded by the towns-
people and their silent children? Does one
mother cluck and tend to one small com-
plaining child who does not understand
the Ceremony? Does that little boy or girl
look to the suspended feet of the people
from away, my wife and I, who cannot speak
except with our wide, white eyes, because
we are gagged and bound fast? Does that
little boy or girl say, "Where's the wood,
Mommy? Where is the wood for the fire?"

And at that moment does some old man
drive up in his truck? Does the crowd part
as he backs in, barely looking in the rear-
view, so assured is he of the dimensions
of his vehicle and his world, this world to
which my wife and I do not belong? Does
he dump out his payload of white oak at
our feet, seasoned three summers in a hot,
dry shed to take fire quick and hungrily
on this morning?

Does he say to the little girl or boy, to
my wife and me, to the town, "There's your
goddamned wood!"?

And then, when it is all done, when the smoke and silent, pointless struggling ends and what's left is cleared away, when the fair opens to the public that first day and an antique tractor stands bright red in the spot where we died, will you all take the peapod back then, and store it for another year? And will your children be safe for that year? Safe from the cold and famished ocean and the clams that sing to them from the bottom of the lake?

None of those things happened, of course. I did not say those things, and my wife and I were not burned alive. I took my mail and went home. Maine is not a death cult. I mean, it is. But it's a slow one. It creeps in like the tide, and without your even noticing, the ground around you is swallowed by water, until it is gone.

By the time we got the peapod in the water, it was getting cold. Leaves were yellowing on the trees, and you could already see the light was lower in the sky. Autumn was arriving. It was August first.

Vacationland

I have been pretty coy so far on the subject of my mother and her death. I was twenty-nine when she died. She was fifty-eight. I had been married to my wife less than a year, but we had been together already for ten. In many ways she had become my mom's daughter too. What more is there to say than it was traumatic, a moment that breaks your life in half? That you never heal from it, and it blankets your life in sadness and fear forever? Not much, except for this little bit.

She had been diagnosed with lung cancer the previous fall. The cancer was as deliberate and strong and persistent as she had always been. By the time she was dying it was spring.

I had been finishing my seventh year working at a literary agency. I loved my colleagues and my clients. I loved an industry that encouraged long lunches and still closed early on Fridays once the summer started sneaking up. But I was unhappy. I wanted to be a writer, and that meant I could not be an agent in good faith and compete with my own clients.

Oh, I also was unhappy because my mom was dying. So one Friday I left work and I did not go back. I went home to help my father take care of her.

She was in a hospital bed at home by then. My father and I would keep her company and watch movies. I do not know whether it was the drugs or the cancer, but her mind had broken by then. She was spacey. She lost track of days and people. She said weird things and got fixated on certain ideas. She became obsessed with going back to New York to see **Cats**, which was still running then. I called about tickets, but all of the wheelchair seats were booked until long after she would surely be gone.

Old friends would come to dinner and we'd eat together around her bed. After eating she would have a cigarette. She had taken up smoking again: it didn't matter anymore. When the old friends said good-bye, they knew it was forever. Night after night this happened, but somehow it didn't feel terrible. Slow death keeps you busy with chores and distractions. I loved the time I spent with her. She had no hair left, just a bit of suede on her scalp. I liked the way it smelled when I kissed her on the head good night. A combination of baby powder and iodine. I've never smelled anything like it since.

When I was little I found a paperback copy of **The Exorcist** in the hall closet. I only read the back cover, and became scared for a full year that I would be possessed by the devil. Possession by the devil was a powerful fantasy for an only child sleeping alone in the top bunk of a bunk bed, with only shadow and empty space below him for company. It didn't matter how good you were, how closely you followed the rules. The devil didn't care. If the devil wanted you, he got you. The girl who is possessed in **The Exorcist** first felt the devil coming when her bed started shaking. I would lie awake at night and wonder when I would feel the first tremor. And soon enough my bed **did** start shaking: it was a rickety bed, and my heart was beating so hard. I went in to see my parents. My father was asleep, but my mom was still awake, reading and smoking. I confessed I was afraid of the devil. She said, "Don't worry. There is no devil."

"There isn't?" I said.

"That's right," she said. She told me then for the first time that she was an atheist. "There can't be a devil, because there is no god." I remember admiring my mother. She was funny and she was honest. But this was not a comfort to me.

After a few weeks caring for my mom at home, I noticed that none of my clients missed me. They wished me well, of course. They cared about me. But to my surprise, their personal and professional lives did not collapse without my being there to tend to them. I was not essential to their world at all.

Eventually my mom declined and she went to the hospital. My dad and I slept in her room. More visitors came. More good-byes were said. At some point I asked her if she was at peace with the idea of dying. She looked at me like I was stupid and insane. "No," she said. "I want to live." **You idiot!** would have finished the sentence nicely. It was one of the only times she seemed really disappointed in me. I realized I had learned everything I know about death from movies. There is no peace in dying.

She was still an atheist, but she had taken

to saying the Lord's Prayer. It was a revisiting of her own lapsed and comforting rituals, and maybe a hedging of her bets. My non-Catholic wife taught her the Protestant add-on to the end: "For thine is the kingdom and the power and the glory, forever and ever. Amen." I still say it from time to time to remember her.

My friend Liz came to town. She was promoting her novel. I asked her if she believed in any form of afterlife. I don't know if she was lying or not, but she said, "Yes. I believe in all of it. I believe in everything." I appreciated her kindness. I wanted to be comforted. But this was not a comfort to me.

One night my father, my wife, and I went back to my parents' house to sleep in non-hospital beds. Liz was still in town. She and my wife and I were sitting in the kitchen talking when the phone rang. I answered. There is no peace in dying, but there is peace when it is done.

I went back to New York, accepted the condolences of my friends and colleagues, and then quit my job. I was back home in Massachusetts within a week. A friend at a magazine assigned me to write an article about cheese for money. I became a professional writer. I spent the summer there with my dad and my wife. I did not cry until the summer was over. We went back to New York, and I started a new life. It was the year 2000.

None of this is anything you needed to know to understand that I am sad my mother died. It's not even worth mentioning, except I have to tell you **that** in order to tell you this. I wish she were alive, but I am grateful for her death. If she were alive, I would likely still be working at the literary agency. For how much longer in my life would I have believed there was time for everything? And by the time I faced my own mortality at the Bookmill in western Massachusetts, how much less would I have done? Her leaving taught me about the worst sadness, one we all must face eventually. I feel lucky I am better equipped to help others who are going through it now.

She left me and my wife a house in rural western Massachusetts. She taught me there is no devil.

She taught me that the world would continue without me. And eventually I learned that lesson. It took some time. It's a tough one for an only child to absorb.

Everything is cliché. Her death taught me that life is short.

When I kissed her head and smelled her scalp one time, near the end of spring and the beginning of summer, she was delusional. She comforted me. "Thank you for visiting me," she said. "Lie down. Get some rest. This is your vacation."

A Little Beyond
the Limits of
Safe Travel

If you have not driven with a small boat trailer attached to your Jeep, this is what it is like. It is easy when you are driving forward. You get used to the extra weight quickly, and you just drive along. The only problem is that it is easy to forget what you are doing. Then you take a turn and you can see in your side-view mirror that you are being followed by some kind of ghost boat that is floating above the road, and you shriek.

Driving backward with the trailer is not easy. Steering in reverse is already an un-natural act requiring years of brain-scarring experience to feel anything close to instinc-tive and unterrifying. But now you are also pushing a long aluminum trailer full of pea-pod behind you, and it is doing the exact opposite of everything you have learned. If you steer right, it goes left. If you line it up perfectly with where you are trying to push it—say the gravelly slope of the landing at the boatyard—and you begin backing up, it veers off to the right due either to tiny micro-angles between the trailer and your hitch or the fact that trailers are inherently assholes. If you attempt to recorrect your course, the laws of physics change. This actually happens: all of natural law reverses and suddenly your peapod is beside you, jackknifed in the boatyard parking lot.

In this scenario, the boatyard is closed for the day, so the parking lot is empty. But there are two men standing at the edge of the parking area, at the foot of the long dock that leads out to the harbor beyond. You don't know this yet—you have never spoken to either of them—but one of them is the owner of the boatyard. He is the son of the famous boat designer who started the boatyard. He is also the grandson of the famous writer. The other is his coworker.

They had been watching ominous clouds over the harbor at the end of the day. But now they are watching you try to do something that not only have you never done before, but you have never really **seen** done. Your best guess is that you are supposed to line up this trailer with the landing, and push the trailer and the boat tied onto it deep into high tide,

where your wife waits now to receive it. You
have to get the whole trailer into the ocean
without also getting your car in the ocean.
You have to do this while being watched by
two men who make boats and launch boats
of every kind and size and have done so probably for one thousand years, because they are
immortal maritime gods, and you are a dumb
Icarus whose wax wings are melting under
their gaze in their parking lot. Even without
the context of this specific scenario, backing
a trailer with a small boat on it into the water
feels like this.

The owner of the boatyard and his coworker watched placidly as I jackknifed the
trailer a second time, and then a third. Their
faces showed neither alarm, nor derision, nor
care. They didn't offer to help me. They would
never help me. My failure in front of their
stone faces would be my punishment for being
from away. I despaired. But then I remembered the lesson of the cairns and did something very unusual for me. I stopped steering,
rolled down my window, and said out loud,
"I do not know what I'm doing."

Their faces immediately broke. I would not

say they broke into smiles, but into a kind of neutral living warmth they could deploy or reserve at will, like androids coming out of sleep mode. "We'll help," they said.

I had misunderstood them completely. They weren't punishing me by not helping, they were respecting my privacy by letting me fuck up on my own. But now that I asked for help, the maritime gods came to my aid.

The coworker didn't take over for me, but showed me how to adjust the wheel properly. The owner of the boatyard monitored my descent to the sea, calling out course corrections, guiding me to my wife, who was waiting like a siren in the tide. But at the end of the maneuver, perhaps sensing the erotic metaphoric charge for which the sea is known, they left us to each other.

As I backed into the landing, I felt my back and neck press into the seat, as gravity shifted, as the sky filled up my windshield. Behind me, unseen, my wife released the boat from the trailer as I mashed the clutch and brake flat to the floor in prayerful neutral. Then she said, "OK," and I eased up on the clutch and released the emergency brake while gassing it gently into first to begin the climb back to land. I don't know how to launch a boat, but I will brag forever about my skill with a manual transmission. I towed the wet skeleton of the unburdened trailer off to a remote corner of the parking area and kicked it.

My wife had rowed the peapod to the dock. When I joined her, her eyes blazed with thrill. She told me that while she was tying up the peapod in the dinghy pen, the owner of the boatyard came by and showed her a new way to tie a bowline knot. I did not know what any of this meant.

"Don't you know how to tie a, uh . . . that knot?" I asked.

"Not well enough!" she said.

It is hard to overstate the disbelief and embarrassment but redeeming excitement my wife felt about this. Imagine meeting the most famous movie star you can think of. Now imagine having dinner with that person. Now imagine that person telling you about the time he went to a Scientology party. Imagine that person explaining he saw a Scientologist attempt to cure another partygoer's injured knee with a "touch assist."

And when you are confused about what that means, imagine that person demonstrating a Scientology touch assist on your wife. Imagine that person touching your wife's shoulder and saying, "Can you feel this?" and your wife saying, "Yes," and that person saying, "Thank you." Then that person is touching your wife's arm and saying, "Can you feel this?" and your wife is saying, "Yes," and the most famous movie star says, "Thank you."

Well, I don't have to imagine this scenario because IT HAPPENED TO ME. My friend Sarah invited us to a play featuring one of Sarah's friends, who happens to be one of the most famous movie stars, and afterward we all went out to dinner, and then the star of many of my favorite movies SCIENTOLOGY-TOUCHED MY WIFE ALL OVER AS I WATCHED, AND IT WAS AMAZING. **That** is how surreal it was for my wife to get an impromptu knots course from the owner of the boatyard, the son of a famous boat designer, and the grandson of her favorite writer.

We could not go far in the peapod. It wasn't designed for distance, but it didn't matter. Things were different on the water. Where

Massachusetts had been my land and Maine, at least the land part, had been hers, the ocean and the little shelter islands that we could reach as our rowing arms grew stronger were new and neutral territory. I would stand up in the boat—because you really could do that . . . you really could break that rule, because the peapod would not tip or fail you— and I would scan the shore. Maine may be full of ambiguities, and its sky full of shades of gray. But it can also be blunt, and sometimes its metaphors can be a little on the nose. So I regret that I must write: I literally had a new point of view.

A typical outing would be to a little island, only a few oar strokes from shore. We would beach the peapod for a moment so that our children could get out. They would go off exploring on their own. You could walk the whole perimeter of the island in an hour, just strolling. But even when your children are older and have demonstrated common sense and physical and emotional resiliency due to your really incredible, award-worthy parenting, you still feel a pang of panic when they leave your sight. I would watch them disappear behind the trees as the shoreline curved off to the right, where they would scamper on slick wet rocks or fall or drown or meet an ill-intentioned stranger or whatever their fate might be.

And then my wife would also leave me, taking the peapod out on a solo row, following her deep, genetic Maine blood—calling to the ocean and misanthropy. I would watch her then disappear as the island curved around to my left, rowing her boat, utterly alone, the happiest I've ever seen her.

They would leave me on the beach, an only child once more, and I would take off my shirt and go swimming. By the end of that summer I had started swimming pretty frequently in the waters of Maine. I would not say that I learned to enjoy it. Even in August, when the water is at its warmest, it is still cold. But I did enjoy learning to endure it.

There are transitions in life whether we want them or not. You get older. You lose jobs and loves and people. The story of your life may change dramatically, tragically, or so quietly you don't even notice. It's never any fun, but it can't be avoided. Sometimes you just have to walk into the cold dark water of the unfamiliar and suffer for a while. You have to go slow, breathe, don't stop, get your head under, and then wait. And soon you get used to it. Soon the pain is gone and you have forgotten it because you are swimming, way out here where it's hard and where you were scared to go, swimming sleekly through the new. That's the gift of a Maine vacation: you survive it.

And in that sense, Maine itself is a metaphor. This is great news for me, because it means that I am technically not a Maine humorist after all. I am a metaphor humorist. And this is also great news for you, because if you get everything you need to from the metaphor, you don't actually have to go to Maine. And this is finally great news for me again, because I don't want to see you there. The spirit of Maine has infected me. I gave you your goddamned wood. Now get the fuck out of here.

Yippee

The first winter I spent in Maine, I was attacked by a barn door. There is a reason people write horror stories set in Maine where bad things happen quickly and sentient barn doors thirst for your blood. It is not full of vampires like I thought (an original idea that only I have ever had), but it is still dangerous and haunted and empty. I have been as far north as Calais, but that is still on the coast. There is a world of dark inland forest beyond that, what one of our year-round neighbors has explored and named a "great disappearing emptiness." And in the winter even the coast feels underpopulated, a dark dream version of what you remember from the summer. The creepiness comes from that quiet, from the gray pall of the sky, from the fog called sea smoke, clinging to the surface of the reach on winter mornings, from the sad stories that sneak out from the shadows.

It was last Christmas, the second year we owned the house. We decided to brave

December there and we had conned Jonathan and Christine and their family into visiting us. When they arrived, snow had fallen fast and thick and our driveway was now an ice bowl. I was shoveling out a path across it, from our house to the garage.

I told you that our house was built to look like it was two hundred years old by a carpenter with missing fingers on his right hand. He also built the garage. Upstairs in the garage was the tidy, modern mother-in-law apartment where the carpenter and his wife had lived when they were building the house, and where we now installed Jonathan and his family. Downstairs was once his workshop. The abandoned outlets and ventilation tubes still stick out of the concrete floor where they once connected to the saws he used to mill the lumber to build the house with his own one-and-a-half hands. True to his fake antique vision the garage was built to look like an old barn, with a great swinging barn door. It latched on the outside with a thick wrought-iron hook that curled to a sharp black point.

I also told you that the carpenter and his wife built this house to grow old in, and

I told you that they changed their mind. I didn't tell you why, but it wasn't a secret. When we walked through the house with him after the closing, the carpenter told the story with the sort of calm of someone who has processed deep loss. He explained that their daughter's fiancé had died while visiting them in Maine a couple of years before.

We were passing from the master bedroom to the upstairs bathroom. It was March, but we could still see snow on the ground through the window on the landing. My wife and I passed a moment of silent, wide-eyed marital telepathy. Did the fiancé die **in the house**? It was ghoulish to ask, and we don't believe in ghosts. But how could we live here without knowing?

But sensing our worry the carpenter reassured us that in fact it all happened far away from here. He explained that his daughter's fiancé drowned on a camping trip. He didn't go into the details. Life did not just end for the fiancé; it was transformed for all of them, from happy vacation to unbearable sadness in one queasy, sad second. We understood.

After that, he explained, their daughter

didn't want to come to Maine anymore. She couldn't. So they were going to start over again, in a new old house—this one **actually** old, in another state in New England. After we completed the final walk-through we said goodbye in the kitchen. The carpenter handed us the keys. "We were hoping you would be the ones who bought our house," they said. "You were **meant** for it." They were very sweet, but it still sounded like a horror movie to me.

Of course the house was not haunted. But as soon as we bought it, the barn-garage seemed to hunger for me. I had already had bad collisions with the electrical outlets in the old workshop. They grow out of the floor, metal boxes blooming on tubular stems, at odd angles. My ankles would keep catching the corners of them. One bit a crescent gash into me that didn't bleed, but also never quite seemed to heal, leaving a scar that looks like a purple, crooked smile. I dodged them again now as I put the snow shovel away and walked back outside. I was tired out and sweating beneath my winter jacket, but the path back to the house was straight and clean, and I felt good about it. I was just about to close the barn door, but the wind did it for me. It whistle-shrieked in the woods across the road, and I turned to listen to it, and then the door blew hard against me, impaling the wrought-iron hook into my forearm, just below the elbow. It went straight through my jacket.

You know when an injury is serious the second it happens. Like when you are stabbed in the arm while standing alone in cold air that carries the happy sounds of your family and friends across the frozen driveway to you. And you know you cannot get to them until you unattach yourself from this barn door. But even then you also pretend that it's fine. You don't want to admit that it's serious. You don't want to admit that the next step is to pull the meat of your body off this iron hook, because who knows what will happen after that?

I did it. The hook made a slight sucking sound as I lifted my arm off it. I felt a warm oozing wetness begin to blossom down my arm. I casually fast-walked along the path, into the house, past my family and the warm fire and into the bathroom where I could take off my jacket in private and see what I had done to myself. Surprisingly my arm was not gushing blood. It was another of the barn-garage's uncanny mystery wounds: a deep, fingerprint-sized hole burrowed into my flesh; I could see muscle and fat where the skin pulled back. But out of it emerged just a slow ooze of reddish lymph. I poured hydrogen peroxide on it and applied pressure until it seemed to slow and added several Band-Aids.

"It's funny," I said when I emerged. "The barn door attacked me with its iron hook! But it's not serious! Ha ha, Happy New Year, I'm fine!" I thought I was.

Jonathan said, "I have my SUV. I bet I could drive you to the doctor."

I said that would not be necessary. "But," I said, "don't we need gin and milk? Let's go to the supermarket!" My brain must have really thought that I was fine and that driving through snowy roads in the increasing dark was really NO BIG DEAL, because we let my daughter come with us.

It is normally a twenty-five-minute drive to the supermarket. Jonathan was driving half speed as new snow began to fall. Finally, my brain gave up its plan to convince my body that everything was fine. I said quietly to Jonathan, "You know what? My sleeve is now full of pus. Would you mind taking me to the hospital?"

"I thought so," said Jonathan.

He dropped me off at the ER of the local hospital. It's a good one, small but modern, with a water view. In his later years, the famous writer would sometimes check himself in there for a little rest and attention. And he died there. I insisted that Jonathan not wait for me but instead backtrack to the supermarket. "Get the milk!" I commanded. "Get the gin!"

The ER waiting room was empty. I could not find anyone to see me. Finally a man swam forward from behind a glass panel and took down my name and insurance information. He told me I was lucky: they weren't very busy that night. In fact, as far as I could tell, I was the evening's only patient. He pointed to the hallway and suggested I walk down it. I did so. I went through one set of doors to another waiting room. Nobody. I was not sure what to do. It was scary. Were there rusty wheelchairs tipped over at the end of the hall? Bedpans full of blood on empty stretchers? Did the fluorescent lights hum and flicker ominously? No. It's a very well-maintained little hospital. But wandering around an abandoned hospital in the middle of a snowstorm while pressing your palm onto your oozing arm-hole was enough to set the horror-movie mood. It felt like I was the last person on Earth. **Finally**, I thought to myself.

But then they collected me: the nurses and physicians' assistants who probably had given up on the night. They emerged from various swinging doors and smiled when they saw that I was not some child with cancer or a man who had opened his face on the kick of his chain saw. This middle-aged dumb dad with a puncture would just be a welcome distraction on a winter night. Not something that would keep them awake for the rest of their lives.

A female nurse in scrubs beamed at me as she inspected my arm-hole. "Yep!" she said. "That's a pretty good laceration!" She seemed excited about it.

It would be just a few stitches and then I'd go home. The nurse sat me down on a bench in an examination room. The paper on the bench was crinkly. She took my medical history. Having been a good and conscientious patient since my mom took me to my first allergist appointment, I knew the drill.

Was I allergic to penicillin?

No.

Any drug sensitivities?

I've always been told not to take ibuprofen, but I do not know why. Something to do with my asthma. It is an enduring mystery.

Do I smoke?

Not anymore.

Do I drink?

Yes.

"Do you drink every day?"

I had never heard this particular question in the medical rundown before. My inclination was to say no, I just drink socially. But socially means every day. Every evening my wife makes us martinis and we talk about our days as I cook dinner and our children ignore us. It is a great pleasure in our lives: this rediscovering of each other as our children age. It is our indulgence. But how do you explain that to a medical professional who clearly is screening for alcoholism? And then I realized I didn't have to. I didn't have to explain anything, because I am a grown-up.

"Yes," I said. "Every day."

And she looked up from her clipboard and said, "Yippee! Me too." This is true.

And then we made out for a little while.

That part is not true—just one more fake fact for old time's sake. What happened instead was a younger, shy guy who turned out to be an MD came back to poke a needle full of anesthetic around my arm-hole to prep for the stitches. Jonathan came back from the supermarket with milk and gin and my daughter. She got to come to my exam room to keep me company. I felt comforted by her. We took pictures of the wound to send to my wife, knowing that they would make her faint.

Finally, Dr. Young Guy got out the curved little needle: a silvery modern miniature of the iron hook that got me. He used it to sew me up. He was nervous, and I wondered how many times he had done it before. My daughter watched closely with interest. The nurse watched him too, probably knowing that she could do a better job.

Then Jonathan drove us back. Our rotten rock road had been plowed again by the time we made the turn off the main road. I saw our neighbor Clark, the retired pastor, on the rotten rock road. He was walking his dog. We waved to each other. I no longer consider my neighbors to be monsters but friends, and Clark seemed glad that we had come to spend some of the winter and the dark with him.

It was only a little farther until we reached our driveway, and then we were home.

ACKNOWLEDGMENTS

This book grew out of stories that I first told in a basement. When I ran out of fake facts to tell, I panicked. It was Mike Birbiglia who suggested that I try what he did: book a bunch of nights at Union Hall in Brooklyn, get up on their basement stage and start talking, and see what comes out. The result was not just this book, but four and a half years of surprising evenings, two one-human touring shows, a sense that the future is not hopeless, and many, many new friends. Along with Mike, I thank the others who helped build that society and kept its secrets: Chenoa Estrada and Kelly Van Valkenburg, Olivia Wingate, Heather D, Marianne Ways, Bex Finch, Hannah Brandeis, Alex Nahas, and everyone at Union Hall.

Later the show moved to a larger location, this one aboveground but closer to the Gowanus Canal. From this era I thank Trish Nelson, Jeffrey Mumm, Carly Henry, Jeff

O'Neill, and all of the staff at the Bell House. Given my schedule, I will probably see all of you tomorrow. And to all the people who came to those shows and my many secret guests, I cannot name you all, so I will only say this: Hail Satan. You know what I mean.

My family was welcomed into two incredible communities in New England, and sadly, this is how I repay them. So as only partial apology, I offer thanks in Massachusetts to David, Cindy and Erin LeBlanc, Sarah Reid and Matthew Latkiewicz, Colette Katsikas, Susan Shilliday and everyone at the Montague Bookmill, and all of the Belmontes: Chris, Melissa, Atticus, Enzo, and Pax. And in Maine I say thank you to Brad and Leslie Fletcher, Heidi Julavits and Ben Marcus, Brian and Karin Larkin, Molly and Eric Blake, Michael Sheahan and Michelle Keyo, Jonathan Lethem and Amy Barrett, Libby and Rick Chamberlain, Basha Burwell and Peter Behrens, Mike and Hannah Nowell, Nancy, Stephanie, and Tracy at the library, Lorinda and Bob at the store, all the children of all these people, everyone at the boatyard and the Skiff Club, Ayelet Waldman and All Those

Chabons (my favorite band), and the Fresh
Banana Man of the I-95 Kennebunk Service
Plaza.

Heidi Feigin made the live tour of **Vacationland** possible, and Ira Glass recorded the
show, which recording I then gave to Kassie
Evashevski, who has helped me so much and
for so long. She gave that recording to Brian
Tart at Viking, who listened to it and believed
it could be a book. His trust in me has always
been so meaningful and also probably un-
wise. To these, and to all the team at Viking:
I am very grateful.

Sean McDonald, let's go to McManus
again soon.

Aaron Draplin surprised and delighted
me by designing this book jacket, and Wyatt
Cenac consulted on it, two geniuses whose
decency and taste I am lucky to benefit from.
And thank you, John Roderick, for coining
the term "privilege comedy."

To Jonathan Coulton and Christine Con-
nor and their children: please come back to
Maine soon.

To my dad, it was scary to know you were
in the audience that time at the Wilbur

Theater in Boston when I was talking about marijuana onstage. But I don't know what I was worried about. You have always been so loving, forgiving, and supportive. I am grateful to you and Adele, and I love you.

And as for my wife and children, I know them personally, so I don't need to thank them here. They are just in the other room right now, and I am lucky that this is true.

That is all.

Jh, June 2017, Brooklyn